CONTENTS

FEAR THE FUTURE

HUMOR HEROES

COMING OF AGE

SO BAD IT'S GOOD

CRIMES AND MISDEMEANORS

MADE AND REMADE

THE HUNGER GAMES

1. *The Hunger Games* **is based on the book by which author?**

    A. Suzanne Collins
    B. Stephenie Meyer
    C. Lois Lowry
    D. J.K. Rowling

2. Which prolific composer, who wrote music for films such as *Pretty Woman,* *The Sixth Sense,* **and** *The Dark Knight,* **wrote the music featured in** *The Hunger Games?*

    A. Hans Zimmer
    B. James Newton Howard
    C. James Horner
    D. Alan Silvestri

3. What is the name of the fictional country in the dystopian future of *The Hunger Games?*

    A. Panamerica
    B. Avox
    C. Panem
    D. The District

ANSWERS

1.   A. Suzanne Collins

Suzanne Collins wrote several children's books before tackling the more mature subject matter of The Hunger Games. *In 2012, Amazon announced that she had sold more Kindle books than any previous author.*

2.   B. James Newton Howard

James Newton Howard has written music for more than 100 films, and has been nominated for eight Academy Awards. He also won a Grammy Award for his work on The Dark Knight, *and an Emmy Award for the television show* Gideon's Crossing.

3.   C. Panem

The name for the fictional country of Panem comes from the phrase "Panem et Circenses," meaning "bread and circuses." This is a reference to the Roman Empire, when citizens were provided superficial, and sometimes violent, entertainment by the government to distract them from their lack of freedom.

QUESTIONS

4. The main character in *The Hunger Games* is named Katniss Everdeen. Where does the name "Katniss" come from?

    A. It is a type of fish
    B. The author made up the name
    C. It is a small mammal
    D. It is a plant

5. Jennifer Lawrence was reportedly paid $500,000 to appear in the first installment of *The Hunger Games*. How much did she make for the next film in the series?

    A. $2 million
    B. $10 million
    C. $500,000
    D. $5 million

6. The dystopian society in the film is divided into sections called districts. What is the main industry in District 12, where Katniss lives?

    A. Coal mining
    B. Hunting
    C. Steel production
    D. Weapons manufacturing

7. Which actress plays the flamboyant Effie Trinket, who accompanies Katniss and her fellow tribute, Peeta Mellark (Josh Hutcherson), to the games?

    A. Julianne Moore
    B. Amy Adams
    C. Elizabeth Banks
    D. Natalie Dormer

ANSWERS

4.   D. It is a plant

Katniss is a plant with white flowers and arrow-shaped leaves. This is fitting, since Katniss Everdeen's weapon of choice is a bow and arrow.

5.   B. $10 million

Interestingly, Jennifer Lawrence was reluctant to accept the role of Katniss Everdeen, because she was afraid of how it would affect her career as an "indie" actress. But after such a large pay raise, it's safe to say the effect on her career was quite positive!

6.   A. Coal mining

Much of the population of District 12 works in coal mines. Although the location of District 12 is never specifically mentioned, the industry and geography seem to suggest it is somewhere in the Appalachians – perhaps Kentucky or West Virginia.

7.   C. Elizabeth Banks

Effie Trinket dresses in the style of the Capitol, which is quite elaborate and intricate. Elizabeth Banks spent 45 minutes a day just having manicures before filming.

QUESTIONS

8. How many tributes are sent to the Capitol to compete in the games?

        A. 30
        B. 24
        C. 12
        D. 20

9. In which installment of the games are Katniss and Peeta forced to compete in *The Hunger Games?*

        A. 75th
        B. 51st
        C. 57th
        D. 74th

10. Who plays the part of Katniss' sympathetic stylist, Cinna?

        A. Woody Harrelson
        B. Stanley Tucci
        C. Lenny Kravitz
        D. Liam Hemsworth

11. All the tributes are given stylists to prepare them for the games. What is the first outfit designed for Katniss by her stylist?

        A. A fiery red ball gown
        B. A dress that appears to be on fire
        C. A reinforced suit for the arena
        D. A simple white dress

ANSWERS

8.   B. 24

Twenty-four "tributes" are chosen from the 12 districts — one boy and one girl from each location.

9.   D. 74ᵗʰ

Including the 22 tributes who die in the 74th year of the games, a total of 1,725 tributes have died in the history of the Hunger Games!

10.   C. Lenny Kravitz

Jennifer Lawrence is a friend of Lenny Kravitz's daughter, Zoë, and as a result, felt uncomfortable calling him by his first name on the set. Because she would only call him "Mr. Kravitz," the entire cast and crew began to refer to him as Mr. Kravitz.

11.   B. A dress that appears to be on fire

Cinna designs a dress that appears to be engulfed in flames, which results in Katniss' nickname of "the girl on fire."

QUESTIONS

12. The cornucopia in the middle of the arena was constructed based on the designs of which architect?

      A. Frank Lloyd Wright
      B. Alden B. Dow
      C. Frank Gehry
      D. I.M. Pei

13. What is the first gift Katniss receives from sponsors when she is in the arena?

      A. Burn ointment
      B. Water
      C. A bow and arrow
      D. Soup

14. What is the name of the poisonous berry the tributes discover in the arena?

      A. Nightshade
      B. Blackberry
      C. Nightberry
      D. Nightlock

ANSWERS

12.   C. Frank Gehry

The modern-looking cornucopia was based on the architecture of Frank Gehry, whose work includes the Guggenheim Museum in Bilbao, Spain, and the Walt Disney Concert Hall in Los Angeles.

13.   A. Burn ointment

Katniss is burned when the Gamekeepers set fire to part of the forest in an attempt to keep her moving through the arena. The ointment heals her wounds surprisingly quickly and helps her to keep competing.

14.   D. Nightlock

Katniss and Peeta discover a dead tribute who has eaten the berries, mistaking them for a safe meal. Later, they both survive the arena by threatening to commit suicide by eating a handful of Nightlock.

QUESTIONS

15. True or false:

Woody Harrelson is never seen eating meat in any of the dining scenes.

16. True or false:

The name of Elizabeth Banks' character is never spoken in the movie.

17. True or false:

Donald Sutherland was initially uninterested in the role of President Snow, but the director of the film convinced him to take the part.

18. The last tribute to die in the arena is _____.

ANSWERS

15. True

Harrelson is a vegetarian, and as a result is only ever seen eating desserts or vegetables in scenes where the characters are eating.

16. True

Although the character of Effie Trinket is an important role in the film, her name is never mentioned.

17. False

Sutherland actually saw the script by accident, and liked it so much that he wrote to director Gary Ross explaining why he would be great for the part.

18. Cato

Alexander Ludwig, the actor who played Cato, worked out for four hours a day with a U.S. Navy Seal to get into shape for his role in the film. No wonder he persevered for so long!

MINORITY REPORT

1. Who directed the movie *Minority Report?*

    A. Ridley Scott
    B. James Cameron
    C. Steven Spielberg
    D. Luc Besson

2. The film is based on a short story by Philip K. Dick. What other futuristic movie was based on one of his stories?

    A. *Total Recall*
    B. *The Matrix*
    C. *Alien*
    D. *Gattaca*

3. Which composer wrote the score for the film?

    A. Hans Zimmer
    B. Danny Elfman
    C. John Williams
    D. James Horner

4. In what year is the film set?

    A. 2022
    B. 2025
    C. 2043
    D. 2054

ANSWERS

1.   C. Steven Spielberg

Spielberg has stated that he took inspiration from John Huston and The Maltese Falcon *to achieve the film noir look of the movie.*

2.   A. *Total Recall*

Minority Report *was originally envisioned as a sequel to* Total Recall. *The screenwriters wanted it to be set on Mars, and were even planning to bring back* Total Recall's *main character, Douglas Quaid. Eventually the project fell apart, and the story was completely rewritten.*

3.   C. John Williams

Williams and Spielberg have often worked together, bringing us some classic movie and musical score pairings such as Jaws, Raiders of the Lost Ark, *and* Jurassic Park.

4.   D. 2054

To achieve a realistic vision of what the future could be like, Spielberg assembled a team of "future experts." These included Neil Gershenfeld, a professor at MIT, and Jaron Lanier, one of the inventors of virtual reality technology.

QUESTIONS

5. Who plays the part of Danny Witwer, the Justice Department official sent to audit the Pre-Crime system?

    A. Max von Sydow
    B. Liam Neeson
    C. Colin Farrell
    D. Ewan McGregor

6. The three "Pre-Cogs" play a pivotal role in the film. Who are they named after?

    A. Their parents
    B. Mystery writers
    C. Famous detectives
    D. Politicians

7. What is the job of the Pre-Cogs?

    A. They read the minds of detainees
    B. They devise methods of punishment
    C. They predict future murders
    D. They write complex policies

8. In the film, what is a "minority report"?

    A. A petty crime
    B. When a citizen files a complaint with Pre-Crime
    C. A raid that goes wrong
    D. When the vision of one Pre-Cog differs from those of the others

9. Which Pre-Cog is the most gifted?

    A. Agatha
    B. Dashiell
    C. Arthur
    D. They are all equally gifted

ANSWERS

5.   C. Colin Farrell

The character of Danny Witwer was written as an American, but Spielberg changed the character to Irish so Farrell wouldn't have to drop his accent.

6.   B. Mystery writers

The Pre-Cogs include twins named Dashiell and Arthur, who were named after Dashiell Hammett and Arthur Conan Doyle, and Agatha, who was named after Agatha Christie. In Philip K. Dick's story, they are named simply Donna, Jerry, and Mike.

7.   C. They predict future murders

The Pre-Cogs see murders before they occur. When they have a premonition about a crime, an automated system creates a ball with the perpetrator's name, and one with the victim's name. If the ball is brown, it means the murder will be premeditated; if it is red, it will be a crime of passion.

8.   D. When the vision of one Pre-Cog differs from the others

Anderton learns from Dr. Iris Hineman, the creator of Pre-Crime, that the Pre-Cogs do not always agree on their version of the future. When one of them has a vision that differs from the others, this is a "minority report."

9.   A. Agatha

When Anderton is framed for a murder he has yet to commit, he removes Agatha from the Pre-Crime building because she is considered the "most talented." It is his hope that she will generate a minority report to prove his innocence.

QUESTIONS

10. What is the name of the man who cares for the Pre-Cogs?

    A. Gideon
    B. Wally
    C. Howard
    D. Fletcher

11. How does one go about changing their identity in the future of *Minority Report*?

    A. By removing fingerprints
    B. They have a chip implanted in their head
    C. With an eyeball transplant
    D. By hacking into a government computer

12. What was the name of the previous owner of Anderton's new eyeballs?

    A. Mr. Yakamoto
    B. Ms. Lewis
    C. Mr. Lundquist
    D. Mr. Singh

13. Which company's communication headsets are used throughout the film?
    A. Samsung
    B. Nokia
    C. AT&T
    D. Motorola

ANSWERS

10.   B. Wally

Daniel London, the actor who played Wally the Caretaker, reprised his role in the short-lived Minority Report *television series in 2015.*

11.   C. With an eyeball transplant

In order for Anderton to evade the authorities, he visits the seedy, grimy residence of Dr. Solomon Eddie (Peter Stormare) to have a new set of eyeballs implanted. Yikes!

12.   A. Mr. Yakamoto

After recovering from his surgery, Anderton walks into a store where his new eyes are scanned. A holographic image pops up and says, "Hello, Mr. Yakamoto! Welcome back to the Gap."

13.   B. Nokia

Nokia reportedly paid $2 million to design headsets for the characters to use in the film. But they weren't the only company with product placement in Minority Report *– Lexus, Burger King, Aquafina, and Guinness were prominently featured as well.*

QUESTIONS

14. The police use small robots to find and scan humans to check their identities. What are they called?

    A. Falcons
    B. Bugs
    C. Monkeys
    D. Spiders

15. According to the Pre-Cogs, what is the name of the man Anderton is supposed to kill?

    A. Leo Crow
    B. Lemar Burgess
    C. Rufus Riley
    D. Howard Marks

16. What is the name of Agatha's mother?

    A. Sarah Marks
    B. Lara Clark
    C. Anne Lively
    D. Katherine James

ANSWERS

14.   D. Spiders

Since the "spiders" are able to detect body heat, Anderton immerses himself into a bath filled with ice water. However, a popping bubble alerts them to his presence, and they manage to perform their retina scan. Fortunately, the eyeball transplant was a success, and the spiders identify him as Mr. Yakamoto.

15.   A. Leo Crow

Anderton is led to believe that Crow kidnapped his son, Sean, yet he chooses not to kill him. Strangely, this decision upsets Crow. The truth is that he was hired to plant evidence implicating him as Sean's kidnapper, in exchange for his family's financial wellbeing after his death.

16.   C. Anne Lively

Anne Lively wanted her daughter back, but the leader of the Pre-Crime program, Lamar Burgess (Max von Sydow), wanted to protect the future of Pre-Crime at any cost. He killed Anne Lively, but staged it in such a way that it would be difficult for the Pre-Cogs to implicate him.

QUESTIONS

17. True or false:

Tom Cruise and Steven Spielberg each made 15 percent more than their usual movie salaries with *Minority Report.*

18. True or false:

Much of the technology envisioned to give the film its futuristic feel is now actually available.

19. True or false:

Tom Cruise was a close match to the John Anderton character in Philip K. Dick's original short story.

ANSWERS

17. False

The actor and director each agreed to waive their salaries to keep the movie's budget under $100 million. Instead, they agreed to 15 percent of the film's gross profit.

18. True

Minority Report *was ahead of its time. Its fictional future included facial recognition technology, personalized advertising, gesture-based user interfaces, and driverless cars — all of which are now part of our reality.*

19. False

In the original story, John Anderton is described as a short, fat, balding man. Not quite the character Tom Cruise brought to life on-screen!

THE RUNNING MAN

1. *The Running Man* was released in 1987, but it is set in a futuristic, totalitarian society. In which years does the action take place?

    A. 2025–2026
    B. 2017–2019
    C. 2100–2103
    D. 2055–2057

2. The film was loosely based on the book of the same name written by Richard Bachman. Surprisingly, the filmmakers had no idea that "Richard Bachman" was a pseudonym for which writer?

    A. John Grisham
    B. Tom Clancy
    C. Robert Ludlum
    D. Stephen King

3. Richard Dawson plays Damon Killian, the host of a disturbing, brutal game show in which convicted criminals must fight for their lives. In real life, what game show is Dawson famous for hosting?

    A. *Jeopardy*
    B. *The Price Is Right*
    C. *Family Feud*
    D. *Wheel of Fortune*

ANSWERS

1.   B. 2017–2019

The film is set between 2017 and 2019, but some of the movie's details are less-than-futuristic. For instance, Richards finds a box full of cassette tapes in Amber Mendez's closet!

2.   D. Stephen King

Producer Rob Cohen actually purchased the rights to The Running Man *before he discovered the real identity of "Richard Bachman."*

3.   C. *Family Feud*

Dawson was the original host of Family Feud, *and in 1978, he won an Emmy for his work on the game show.*

QUESTIONS

4. Ben Richards, played by Arnold Schwarzenegger, is falsely accused of what crime?

    A. Stealing government property
    B. Firing into a crowd of people rioting for food
    C. Killing a police officer
    D. Kidnapping his brother's girlfriend

5. After Richards escapes from prison, he heads to Los Angeles to get help from his brother. Who does he find living in his brother's apartment?

    A. Amber Mendez, a composer for the network that produces *The Running Man*
    B. A police officer who immediately arrests him
    C. Damon Killian, who offers to put him on the show instead of calling the police
    D. No one – the apartment is eerily empty

6. The suits worn by the contestants on the *Running Man* show have the logo of which athletic shoe company on them?

    A. Nike
    B. Reebok
    C. Adidas
    D. Puma

7. The gladiators who pursue the contestants are known by what name?

    A. Reapers
    B. Mercenaries
    C. Trackers
    D. Stalkers

ANSWERS

4.   B. Firing into a crowd of people rioting for food

Richards is framed after he refuses to carry out the order to shoot into the crowd. He later manages to escape from prison with two friends, William Laughlin (Yaphet Kotto) and Harold Weiss (Marvin J. McIntyre), who are also forced to appear on the show-in-a-show The Running Man.

5.   A. Amber Mendez, a composer for the network that produces
The Running Man

When Richards asks Amber Mendez what happened to his brother, she says that all she knows is that the last tenant of the apartment was taken away for "re-education." We can assume that this is not a good fate for someone in the dystopian future of The Running Man.

6.   C. Adidas

The famous logo appears at the hip and the right arm of the suits the contestants wear.

7.   D. Stalkers

Each "Stalker" has a specific weapon for attacking contestants, such as a flamethrower or a chainsaw. But one by one, Richards assures they get a taste of their own medicine.

QUESTIONS

8. How many square blocks make up the "Game Zone" of the *Running Man* show?

      A. 400
      B. 50
      C. 100
      D. 500

9. Just before Killian sends Richards into the Game Zone, Arnold Schwarzenegger delivers his signature line, "I'll be back." What is Killian's response?

      A. Maybe if you're lucky.
      B. Only in a rerun.
      C. In your dreams.
      D. Over my dead body.

10. Killian uses his hosting charms to stir up the studio spectators, and asks members of the audience to choose those who will go into the Game Zone to hunt down the contestants. Who is the first gladiator to be chosen?

      A. Buzzsaw
      B. Subzero
      C. Fireball
      D. Dynamo

11. In addition to Maria Conchita Alonzo and Dweezil Zappa, which other musician makes an appearance in the movie?

      A. David Bowie
      B. Tom Petty
      C. Mick Fleetwood
      D. Phil Collins

ANSWERS

8.   A. 400

Damon Killian explains to his studio audience that "the Game Zone is divided into four hundred square blocks, left over from the big quake of '97."

9.   B. Only in a rerun.

Schwarzenegger's famous line, which was originally delivered in The Terminator, *was chosen to be #37 on the American Film Institute's "AFI's 100 Years... 100 Movie Quotes" list in 2005.*

10.   B. Subzero

Subzero has his own ice rink in the Game Zone, where he and Richards have a chilly showdown. The studio audience is stunned when Subzero becomes the first gladiator to ever die on the Running Man *game show.*

11.   C. Mick Fleetwood

Mick Fleetwood of Fleetwood Mac plays the leader of the underground resistance. One of his men, played by Dweezil Zappa, is named Stevie – obviously a reference to Stevie Nicks of Fleetwood Mac.

QUESTIONS

12. At the end of the film, Killian's imposing bodyguard, Sven, shows up just as Richards is confronting Killian. What does Sven do to Richards?

      A. Straps him into the chair to send him back to the Game Zone
      B. Punches him in the face
      C. Holds him at gunpoint
      D. Nothing

13. True or false:

The winners of past *Running Man* episodes are sent to sunny Hawaii and live lives of luxury.

14. True or false:

The Running Man was the inspiration for the television show *American Gladiators*.

15. True or false:

Jennifer Lopez choreographed the dance number at the start of the *Running Man* show.

16. True or false:

In addition to the *Running Man* show, we're also given a glimpse of another disturbing reality show from this dystopian future called *Climbing for Dollars*.

17. True or false:

The gladiator Dynamo's singing was dubbed in by a professional opera singer.

ANSWERS

12.   D. Nothing

Earlier in the film, a rude, sarcastic Killian suggests that his bodyguard is on steroids. When Sven shows up at the end of the movie, Killian clearly thinks he's about to help. But instead, Sven merely says, "I've got to score some steroids," and walks away, leaving Killian alone to his fate.

13. False

Although the audience is shown footage of past contestants enjoying their time in Hawaii, Richards and Mendez discover the video has been doctored when they find the bodies of the "winners" in the Game Zone.

14. True

American Gladiators *creator John Ferraro was inspired to create a show where contestants competed against "gladiators" in physical challenges on an obstacle course. Fortunately, all the contestants on* American Gladiators *survived unscathed!*

15. False

Although Jennifer Lopez is known for her dancing, it was Paula Abdul who acted as choreographer for the film. Coincidentally, Abdul is also credited with creating the "running man" dance move, which was popular in the '80s.

16. True

In the movie, we see a short clip of Climbing for Dollars, *where a man climbs a rope covered with money as vicious dogs growl and bark on the ground. As he falls off the rope, the screen cuts to a message that says, "*Climbing for Dollars *will be right back."*

17. False

Erland van Lidth, the actor who played Dynamo, was a trained opera singer who performed his own singing in the film.

QUESTIONS

18. True or false:

Arnold Schwarzenegger was unacquainted with any of his costars before the film.

19. Ben Richards was nicknamed the Butcher of _____.

20. Two of the actors from *The Running Man* went on to become state governors:

_____ became the governor of Minnesota, and _____ was voted the governor of California.

ANSWERS

18. False

Schwarzenegger knew at least two of the actors in the movie, Franco Columbu and Sven-Ole Thorsen. In fact, they were both in the wedding party when he married Maria Shriver.

19. Bakersfield

When the movie opens, Richards is flying in a helicopter over Bakersfield, California, where people oppressed by the totalitarian government have resorted to rioting for food. Although he refuses to carry out his orders to fire on them, footage is later doctored to make it appear as if he massacred scores of innocent people, leading to his unfortunate moniker.

20. Jesse Ventura, Arnold Schwarzenegger

Not only were Jesse Ventura and Arnold Schwarzenegger both governors, but they also appeared in three films together: The Running Man, Predator, *and* Batman and Robin.

TOTAL
RECALL

. . . .

1. In what year was the futuristic action movie *Total Recall* released?

    A. 1988
    B. 1989
    C. 1990
    D. 1991

2. Arnold Schwarzenegger plays Douglas Quaid, a man who dreams of a journey to Mars. How does the character differ from the writers' original concept?

    A. In the first draft, Quaid was a woman
    B. He was originally an average-looking accountant
    C. He was supposed to be an alien
    D. Quaid was going to be the villain throughout the film

3. Who directed *Total Recall*?

    A. Paul Verhoeven
    B. John McTiernan
    C. James Cameron
    D. Paul Michael Glaser

ANSWERS

1.   C. 1990

Ronald Shusett and Dan O'Bannon, who wrote the screenplay for Total Recall, *actually began work on the movie in the 1970s, but realized it would be too costly and difficult to make at that time.*

2.   B. He was an average-looking accountant

Originally, Douglas Quaid was written to be an average, accountant-type office worker who dreams of a more exciting life. But Schwarzenegger liked the movie's concept so much that he convinced the producer to tweak the script so he would fit into the role.

3.   A. *Paul Verhoeven*

Schwarzenegger was so impressed with Verhoeven's work on RoboCop *that he specifically requested him to direct* Total Recall.

QUESTIONS

4. Which composer, known for his work on *Alien, Star Trek: The Motion Picture,* and *Poltergeist,* also wrote the music for *Total Recall?*

    A. James Newton Howard
    B. Jerry Goldsmith
    C. Howard Shore
    D. Bill Conti

5. Which *Star Trek* actor provides the voice for the Johnny Cab that Quaid uses on Earth?

    A. Brent Spiner
    B. Avery Brooks
    C. Robert Picardo
    D. Ethan Phillips

6. When Quaid goes to Rekall and asks for the implanted memories of a Mars trip, what planet does the salesman suggest instead?

    A. Saturn
    B. Venus
    C. Neptune
    D. Jupiter

7. Sharon Stone, who plays Quaid's wife, Lori, was inducted as an honorary member into what group because of her work in *Total Recall?*

    A. Association of Space Explorers
    B. Stunt Woman Association
    C. American Martial Arts Organization
    D. The Mars Society

ANSWERS

4.   B. Jerry Goldsmith

Goldsmith was inspired by Basil Poledouris' score in Conan the Barbarian, *which was, incidentally, another film in which Arnold Schwarzenegger starred. Goldsmith considered* Total Recall *one of his best film scores.*

5.   C. Robert Picardo

Robert Picardo played the haughty, affable holographic doctor on Star Trek: Voyager. *His likeness was also used as the model for the Johnny Cab robot's face.*

6.   A. Saturn

The salesman at Rekall tells Quaid that he'd be "much happier with one of our Saturn cruises," but Quaid insists on going to Mars.

7.   B. Stunt Woman Association

Even Arnold Schwarzenegger was impressed with the work Stone put into preparing for her role. On the set, he referred to her as the "Female Terminator."

QUESTIONS

8. What is the name of the cab driver who helps Quaid when he first arrives on Mars?

    A. Robbie
    B. Reggie
    C. Carlos
    D. Benny

9. Which hotel does Quaid check into on Mars?

    A. Holiday Inn
    B. Best Western
    C. Marriott
    D. Hilton

10. When Quaid is confronted by Lori and Dr. Edgemar, how does he come to the conclusion that he is not dreaming?

    A. Lori calls him Hauser instead of Quaid
    B. He pinches himself
    C. He sees a bead of sweat on Dr. Edgemar's forehead
    D. He never sees Lori in his dreams

11. What is the name of the rebel leader on Mars?

    A. Cohaagen
    B. Kuato
    C. Richter
    D. Quad

ANSWERS

8.   D. Benny

At first, Benny seems to be a nice guy, building a rapport with Quaid and helping him escape henchmen. But eventually, Benny turns on Quaid and attempts to kill the leader of the resistance.

9.   D. Hilton

Quaid receives a startling message from his alter-ego, Hauser, who tells him to check into the hotel with a fake ID. Quaid – and the audience – are left to wonder what is real and what is a dream.

10.   C. He sees a bead of sweat on Dr. Edgemar's forehead

Quaid threatens to shoot Dr. Edgemar, who says that it won't matter since it's a dream. But when Quaid notices a bead of sweat on the nervous man's forehead, he concludes that a "dream" person wouldn't be sweating nervously.

11.   B. Kuato

The name Kuato was derived from the Spanish word "cuate," which means "twin." As Quaid discovers, Kuato is a mutant who is easily hidden because he's attached to the stomach of another rebel fighter!

QUESTIONS

12. How many puppeteers were needed to bring the mutant rebel leader to life?

      A. 5
      B. 7
      C. 12
      D. 15

13. In the hotel safe, Quaid discovers a flyer that says, "For a good time ask for _____."

14. At the end of the movie, Quaid tells the evil Mars administrator, "You got what you want. Give these people _____!"

15. True or false:

    Arnold Schwarzenegger escaped a terrible case of food poisoning on the Mexican set because of his insistence that all his food be catered from the U.S.

16. True or false:

    Paul Verhoeven wanted to make sure the audience knew the ending was reality, so he filmed it in a way that there would be no question.

ANSWERS

12.   D. 15

A total of 15 puppeteers were used to control Kuato, who, at the time, looked impressively realistic. According to the director, the special effects designer did such a good job with the puppet that people approached actor Marshall Bell on the street to ask if the puppet appendage was real.

13. Melina

When Quaid is told that he left the handwritten note in the safe himself, he borrows the hotel clerk's pen and writes "Melina" on the flyer, to make sure it matches the handwriting. Since it does, he deduces that he left himself the note.

14. Air

In the scene where the air to the Mars colony is cut off, the director originally envisioned the actors violently gasping for air. But this gave the scene an unintended comic appearance. Instead, the actors were instructed to simply lie down quietly, as if drained of energy, which gave the scene the dramatic feel the director wanted.

15. True

With the exception of Schwarzenegger and producer Ronald Shusett, the entire cast and crew was afflicted with food poisoning. Three years prior, Schwarzenegger had gotten ill on the set of Predator, *which was also filmed in Mexico, which is why he took such extreme cautions with his food!*

16. False

Verhoeven actually wanted the ending to be ambiguous, so we never know if the ending is real or if everything was a dream. This is why the movie simply fades to white at the end.

QUESTIONS

17. True or false:

The film originally had a PG-13 rating, but the filmmakers wanted to make some of the action scenes more violent, which led to an R rating.

18. True or false:

Sharon Stone was cast in *Basic Instinct* due to her performance in *Total Recall.*

19. True or false:

The writers of *Total Recall,* Ronald Shusett and Dan O'Bannon, are also known for their work on 1979's *Alien.*

ANSWERS

17. False

The original cut of the film was actually so violent and gory that it earned an X rating. Since this was not conducive to commercial success, the filmmakers softened the graphically violent scenes to achieve an R rating.

18. True

Paul Verhoeven offered Stone the part in Basic Instinct *after observing her ability in* Total Recall *to switch from an innocent, sweet character to a conniving, sinister character at a moment's notice.*

19. True

Shusett and O'Bannon were actually working on Total Recall *first, but realized that the special effects of the late 1970s wouldn't do justice to the film. Instead, they shelved the idea for more than ten years, and poured their energy into the critically acclaimed* Alien.

ANCHORMAN:
THE LEGEND OF RON BURGUNDY

1. Who plays the title character in the 2004 comedy *Anchorman: The Legend of Ron Burgundy*?

    A. Steve Carrell
    B. Will Ferrell
    C. Ben Stiller
    D. Vince Vaughn

2. Who directed the film?

    A. Danny Leiner
    B. John Fortenberry
    C. Adam McKay
    D. Judd Apatow

3. The story was partly inspired by a biography of which journalist?

    A. Barbara Walters
    B. Gloria Steinem
    C. Christiane Amanpour
    D. Jessica Savitch

ANSWERS

1.   B. Will Ferrell

Will Ferrell actually majored in sports journalism at the University of Southern California, but he quickly realized that a career in comedy would be more fun than a career in broadcasting.

2.   C. Adam McKay

Adam McKay and Will Ferrell have quite the comedy partnership. They created the website "Funny or Die," and co-wrote Anchorman, Talladega Nights: The Ballad of Ricky Bobby, *and* Step Brothers.

3.   D. Jessica Savitch

Ferrell says he was watching a biography about Savitch, who was one of the first women to anchor a news broadcast, and he was struck by the level of sexism she had to endure. It inspired him to create the hilarious, yet sexist, characters in the movie.

QUESTIONS

4. For which city does Ron anchor the news?

    A. Los Angeles
    B. San Francisco
    C. San Diego
    D. Las Vegas

5. In which decade does the story take place?

    A. 1960s
    B. 1970s
    C. 1980s
    D. 1990s

6. Who plays Ron's rival and romantic interest, Veronica Corningstone?

    A. Christina Applegate
    B. Tina Fey
    C. Christine Taylor
    D. Leslie Mann

7. What is the name of the cologne that Brian Fantana (Paul Rudd) uses in an attempt to woo Veronica?

    A. Stag
    B. Sex Panther
    C. Kolonia
    D. Wood Grains

ANSWERS

4.   C. San Diego

Ron anchors the news for KVWN Channel 4 news in San Diego. His famous sign-off is "You stay classy, San Diego."

5.   B. 1970s

Although the exact year is never mentioned, there are clues to the timeline. For example, the news team sings a spontaneous verse of "Afternoon Delight," which was popular in 1976, and Champ Kind makes a reference to Gene Tenace, who played for the Padres from 1977 to 1980. Therefore, we can assume the story takes place in the late '70s.

6.   A. Christina Applegate

Christina Applegate is best known for her ten-year stint as the ditzy Kelly Bundy on the television show Married with Children *– a far cry from smart, sassy Veronica Corningstone.*

7.   B. Sex Panther

The cologne is called "Sex Panther by Odion," and according to Brian, it "contains real bits of panther." Not only that, but "60 percent of the time it works every time." It did not, however, work to seduce Veronica.

QUESTIONS

8. What instrument does Ron play?

    A. Bass guitar
    B. Piano
    C. Tenor sax
    D. Jazz flute

9. Which actor plays station manager Ed Harken?

    A. Martin Mull
    B. Fred Willard
    C. Kurtwood Smith
    D. Christopher Lloyd

10. What does Ron's apartment smell like?

    A. Mahogany
    B. Scotch
    C. Vanilla incense
    D. Leather and musk

11. What is the name of Ron's dog?

    A. Dexter
    B. Ralph
    C. Walter
    D. Baxter

ANSWERS

8.   D. Jazz flute

Ron plays in the style of Jethro Tull lead singer and flutist Ian Anderson. For the film, the flute solo was recorded by professional flutist Katisse Buckingham.

9.   B. Fred Willard

Willard is known for his ability to retain his stoic composure even when filming comedies. But he has admitted that Anchorman *proved to be too funny even for him, and the director was forced to stop filming a scene so Willard could finish laughing.*

10.   A. Mahogany

When Ron first meets Veronica, he tries to impress her by saying, "I'm very important. I have many leather-bound books and my apartment smells of rich mahogany."

11.   D. Baxter

Ron's furry companion is named after Ted Baxter, the anchor played by Ted Knight on The Mary Tyler Moore Show.

QUESTIONS

12. Which actor does NOT have a cameo as a rival news anchor in the film?

    A. Tim Robbins
    B. Ben Stiller
    C. Owen Wilson
    D. Vince Vaughn

13. What surprising weapon does Brick (Steve Carrell) use to kill someone?

    A. Bazooka
    B. Samurai sword
    C. Flamethrower
    D. Trident

14. Who has a cameo as a disgruntled biker who kicks Ron's beloved dog off a bridge?

    A. Jack Black
    B. Seth Rogen
    C. Jason Segel
    D. Charlie Hunnam

15. What does Ron exclaim when the biker crashes near his car?

    A. Great Odin's raven!
    B. Knights of Columbus, that hurts!
    C. Antony and Cleopatra!
    D. Son of a bee sting!

ANSWERS

12.   C. Owen Wilson

Although Owen Wilson does not appear in the movie, his brother, Luke, makes an appearance as rival news anchor Frank Vitchard.

13.   D. Trident

After the fight between the news teams that "escalated quickly," the team talks about what happened. Brick recalls, "there were horses, and a man on fire, and I killed a guy with a trident." Ron tells him he should find a safe place to stay, since he's "probably wanted for murder."

14.   A. Jack Black

Jack Black plays a biker who is riding next to Ron's car when Ron tosses a burrito out the window. The burrito causes him to lose control of his motorcycle and crash, and he vindictively kicks Ron's dog off a bridge. But not to worry — Baxter is quite resourceful and returns later in the story!

15.   C. Antony and Cleopatra!

Although Ron uses all of these exclamations during the film, he yells, "Antony and Cleopatra!" as he slams the brakes of his car to check on the biker.

QUESTIONS

16. Who saves Ron and Veronica from the bears at the zoo?

    A. Brick
    B. Baxter
    C. A rival anchor
    D. A fan

17. True or false:

The face-off between the news teams was meant to parody *West Side Story*.

18. True or false:

Amy Poehler had a part in the film that was completely cut out.

19. True or false:

The name of the Mexican restaurant that Veronica visits with the women from the station is called "Escupimos en su Alimento," which means, "eat somewhere else."

20. Complete the quote

(Ron speaking to Brian Fantana from a phone booth): I'm in a
_____!

ANSWERS

16.   B. Baxter

Baxter triumphantly returns after his adventure in the wild, where he befriended several bears and learned to speak their language. His talent with linguistics comes as no surprise, since according to Ron, Baxter also speaks Spanish.

17. True

The fight between the anchors was a nod to the rumble between the Jets and the Sharks. There's even a brick wall covered with graffiti and the number "9" to mark the territory of the rival Channel 9 news team.

18. True

Poehler's part as a disgruntled bank teller was left on the cutting room floor. However, she was given a role in Anchorman 2: The Legend Continues *to make up for it.*

19. False

The truth is much worse, as the name translates to "we spit in your food."

20. Glass Case of Emotion

Ron is so distraught after the biker kicks Baxter off the bridge that he wails incoherently to his friend on the phone. When Brian asks him where he is, Ron replies with the famous quote.

GROUNDHOG DAY

1. Who directed the 1993 movie *Groundhog Day,* in which Bill Murray's character, Phil Connors, lives the same day over and over?

      A. Ivan Reitman
      B. Harold Ramis
      C. Richard Donner
      D. Frank Oz

2. Who was the director's original choice for the part of Phil?

      A. Tom Hanks
      B. Dan Aykroyd
      C. Chevy Chase
      D. Steve Martin

3. Who plays Phil's news producer, Rita?

      A. Michelle Pfeiffer
      B. Madeleine Stowe
      C. Andie MacDowell
      D. Geena Davis

ANSWERS

1.   B. Harold Ramis

Ramis and Murray worked together on numerous projects before Groundhog Day, *including* Caddyshack, Stripes, *and* Ghostbusters.

2.   A. Tom Hanks

Tom Hanks was the first choice for the role of Phil, but the director decided that he would be "too nice" to fit the part.

3.   C. Andie MacDowell

Andie MacDowell had to get the go-ahead from the director to speak with her natural South Carolina accent, which was quite heavy. In fact, in her first film, Greystoke: The Legend of Tarzan, Lord of the Apes, *all of her lines were dubbed by Glenn Close because of her accent.*

QUESTIONS

4. What is the name of the location where Punxsutawney Phil makes his yearly weather prediction?

     A. Punxsutawney Pond
     B. Groundhog Hollow
     C. Pennsylvania Park
     D. Gobbler's Knob

5. For which television station does Phil forecast the weather?

     A. Channel 2 in Philadelphia
     B. Channel 4 in Erie
     C. Channel 7 in Harrisburg
     D. Channel 9 in Pittsburgh

6. One of the groundhog officials is played by actor Bryan Doyle-Murray. What is his relation to Bill Murray?

     A. Brother
     B. Father
     C. Cousin
     D. They are no relation

7. What is the name of the diner where Phil and Rita meet?

     A. Café on the Square
     B. Tip Top Café
     C. Doris' Diner
     D. Waffle Palace

ANSWERS

4.   **D. Gobbler's Knob**

Gobbler's Knob is a real location in Punxsutawney, Pennsylvania. But unlike the movie, which suggests that it is located downtown, the actual Gobbler's Knob is in a remote clearing a couple miles outside of town.

5.   **D. Channel 9 in Pittsburgh**

Phil and Rita, along with cameraman Larry (Chris Elliott), are with WPBH-TV 9 in Pittsburgh.

6.   **A. Brother**

Bill Murray has five brothers, including actors Bryan, Joel, and John, and business-men Andy and Ed.

7.   **B. Tip Top Café**

While Phil is stuck in his Groundhog Day *loop, he returns to the Tip Top café daily, where he gets to know the employees and patrons.*

QUESTIONS

8. What is the song playing on the radio when Phil wakes up every morning?

       A. "Stop! In the Name of Love"
       B. "Do You Believe in Magic?"
       C. "I Got You Babe"
       D. "My Girl"

9. What two things do Phil and Rita toast to at the bar?

       A. Long life and friendship
       B. The groundhog and world peace
       C. Friendship and world peace
       D. Punxsutawney and Pittsburgh

10. What is the name of the insurance salesman who Phil encounters every day?

       A. Felix
       B. Gus
       C. Larry
       D. Ned

11. What kind of poetry did Rita study in college?

       A. Shakespearean sonnets
       B. 19th century French
       C. 20th century American
       D. Japanese haiku

ANSWERS

8. C. "I Got You Babe"

Phil seems doomed to hear the Sonny and Cher song "I Got You Babe" every morning for eternity. The song was #1 in the U.S. for three weeks in August of 1965.

9. B. The groundhog and world peace

Once Phil discovers Rita's favorite drink – sweet vermouth on the rocks with a twist – he proposes a toast to the groundhog. Rita replies that she always toasts to world peace, so during Phil's next time loop, he toasts to world peace.

10. D. Ned

Ned Ryerson runs into Phil on the street and tries to jog his memory about their time together in high school. Ned reminds him that he did a "whistling bellybutton trick" at the school talent show, had a bad case of shingles, and "I dated your sister Mary Pat a couple times until you told me not to anymore."

11. B. 19th century French

The first time Rita tells Phil that she studied 19th century French poetry in college, he laughs. So on his next go-around, he makes sure to impress her by reciting a poem in French. Incidentally, the lines he recites in the film were actually penned by the movie's co-writer, Danny Rubin.

QUESTIONS

12. How much money does Phil offer the piano teacher for a lesson?

    A. $1000
    B. $100
    C. $500
    D. $250

13. What is Rita's favorite flavor of ice cream?

    A. Vanilla
    B. Chocolate
    C. Pistachio
    D. Rocky Road

14. What is the name of the song that plays during the final scene of the film?

    A. I Only Have Eyes for You
    B. It Had to be You
    C. Almost Like Being in Love
    D. Unforgettable

15. True or false:

Bill Murray needed rabies injections while he was working on *Groundhog Day*.

16. True or false:

The movie was filmed on location in Punxsutawney, Pennsylvania.

ANSWERS

12.   A. $1000

Since he lives the same day over and over, Phil spends time observing the details of the day. He discovers a way to steal a bag of money from an armored truck, so is able to pay a large sum of money for his "one" lesson day after day.

13.   D. Rocky Road

Once again, Phil takes note of Rita's likes and dislikes so he can attempt to impress her. Rita comes back to his hotel room, where he has a pint of rocky road ice cream chilling on the frigid windowsill. When she says that she loves rocky road, Phil replies, "yeah, I thought so."

14.   C. Almost Like Being in Love

The song "Almost Like Being in Love" is from the Alan Jay Lerner and Frederick Loewe musical "Brigadoon," which is about a magical Scottish village that only appears once every 100 years.

15. True

Murray was bitten by his groundhog co-star twice, and had to endure preventive injections.

16. False

Groundhog Day was actually filmed in Woodstock, Illinois. There are now plaques marking several shooting locations, including the corner where Ned runs into Phil, and the curb where Phil continually steps into the puddle.

QUESTIONS

17. True or false:

The morning radio announcers were voiced by an actual Chicago radio duo.

18. True or false:

We never discover exactly why Phil was doomed to repeat one day over and over.

19. Finish the quote:

"Okay, campers, rise and shine! And don't forget your booties, cause it's cold out there! It's cold out there every day. What is this, _____?"

ANSWERS

17. False

Although director Harold Ramis asked Chicago talk show host Steve Dahl and his on-air partner to be the voices on the radio, Dahl's partner turned down the part. Instead, the radio hosts were voiced by Ramis and Bryan Doyle-Murray.

18. True

In an early draft of the screenplay, the writers explained that Phil was cursed by a former lover. But ultimately, the filmmakers decided the story worked better if the cause of Phil's predicament remained a mystery.

19. Miami Beach

Phil hears these words from the radio announcers every morning when he repeats his loop. He even attempts to destroy the clock radio, but of course it simply returns to normal when the day starts over. It's not until he hears the announcers say something different that he realizes he is finally out of his Groundhog Day loop.

THE PRINCESS BRIDE

1. Who wrote the original 1973 book *The Princess Bride,* on which the film is based?

    A. James Goldman
    B. William Styron
    C. John Irving
    D. William Goldman

2. Who directed the film?

    A. Mike Nichols
    B. Rob Reiner
    C. Nora Ephron
    D. Ron Howard

3. Who plays the bedridden grandson, who is certain he won't enjoy the book his grandfather plans to read to him?

    A. Fred Savage
    B. Lukas Haas
    C. Jason Bateman
    D. Macaulay Culkin

ANSWERS

1.   **D. William Goldman**

William Goldman started his career as a novelist, and then turned to screenplays. He won two Academy Awards for his work, for Butch Cassidy and the Sundance Kid *and* All the President's Men. *But he has stated that* The Princess Bride *has garnered more responses than any of his other works, saying, "Something in* The Princess Bride *affects people."*

2.   **B. Rob Reiner**

Also known for his work on Stand By Me *and* A Few Good Men, *Reiner first read* The Princess Bride *when he was starring on* All In the Family *in the 1970s.*

3.   **A. Fred Savage**

Fred Savage appeared as the skeptical grandson in The Princess Bride *a year before he began his famous stint as Kevin Arnold on* The Wonder Years.

QUESTIONS

4. The grandfather who reads the book serves as the story's narrator. Which actor plays the part?

       A. Gregory Peck
       B. Jerry Stiller
       C. Peter Falk
       D. Jack Nicholson

5. Which actress plays the part of Buttercup?

       A. Cate Blanchett
       B. Monica Bellucci
       C. Carrie Fisher
       D. Robin Wright

6. What is Westley's response to anything Buttercup asks of him?

       A. It shall be done
       B. As you wish
       C. As you require
       D. Yes m'lady

7. When Buttercup tries to escape from Vizzini and jumps out of the boat, what does Vizzini warn her about?

       A. Giant whales
       B. Man-eating piranhas
       C. Shrieking eels
       D. Fearsome fishes

ANSWERS

4.   C. Peter Falk

At first, 60-year-old Falk thought he looked too young to play the role, and he even thought he should wear aging prosthetics. But he ultimately decided against them.

5.   D. Robin Wright

The Princess Bride *was Wright's film debut. In fact, at the time, 11-year-old Fred Savage was more well known than many in the cast. Cary Elwes (Westley) was an unknown, and Mandy Patinkin (Inigo Montoya) was famous solely to fans of Broadway.*

6.   B. As you wish

Westley answers any request with "as you wish," which, the narrator tells us, is his way of saying "I love you." Later, when Buttercup believes Westley to be the Dread Pirate Roberts, she tells him he can die and pushes him down a hill. Westley replies with his usual "as you wish," and Buttercup realizes she's just shoved the love of her life down a hill.

7.   C. Shrieking eels

The "shrieking eels" were a peril created for the film. In the original novel, Vizzini warns Buttercup about sharks – a decidedly less unusual creature to encounter in the ocean.

QUESTIONS

8. What is the word that Vizzini repeatedly says?

    A. Inconceivable
    B. Impossible
    C. Inexcusable
    D. Irredeemable

9. Who played the role of Fezzik?

    A. Arnold Schwarzenegger
    B. André the Giant
    C. Kareem Abdul-Jabbar
    D. Richard Kiel

10. What are the names of the two rival kingdoms in the film?

    A. Florence and Guild
    B. Flower and Gulch
    C. Florin and Guilder
    D. Fickle and Guile

11. Where does the poison iocane powder come from?

    A. Australia
    B. Brazil
    C. New Zealand
    D. India

ANSWERS

8.   A. Inconceivable

"Inconceivable" seems to be Vizzini's favorite word. He says it so often that Inigo eventually muses, "You keep using that word. I do not think it means what you think it means."

9.   B. André the Giant

Although Schwarzenegger, Abdul-Jabbar, and Kiel were all considered, the role of the giant Fezzik went to the aptly named professional wrestler André the Giant.

10.   C. Florin and Guilder

The names of the rival kingdoms were taken from the names of a former Dutch currency, which was known as both a Florijn and a Gulden. The names were a subtle joke suggesting that the two kingdoms were basically interchangeable.

11.   A. Australia

While Vizzini stalls for time before drinking from a possibly poison-laced cup, he chatters about how the fictional "iocane powder" comes from Australia. In the end, his choice of cup doesn't matter, since Westley spent his years as a pirate building up an immunity to iocane and poisoned both cups.

QUESTIONS

12. Which actor plays the medicine man, Miracle Max?

    A. Robin Williams
    B. John Cleese
    C. Bill Murray
    D. Billy Crystal

13. What is Miracle Max's diagnosis of Westley?

    A. Partly dead
    B. Mostly dead
    C. Barely dead
    D. Completely dead

14. How many times does Mandy Patinkin repeat his famous line, "Hello. My name is Inigo Montoya. You killed my father. Prepare to die"?

    A. Four
    B. Five
    C. Six
    D. Seven

15. What does Fezzik find at the end of the film to help the group escape the castle?

    A. Two wheelbarrows
    B. Four white horses
    C. A cloak
    D. Four silver swords

ANSWERS

12.   D. Billy Crystal

Billy Crystal improvised much of his performance as Miracle Max, which report-edly made the cast and crew laugh so hard they literally hurt. Mandy Patinkin has said that the only injury he suffered on the set was a bruised rib from holding back laughter during Crystal's scenes. And even the director had to leave the set because his constant laughter was making him nauseated!

13.   B. Mostly dead

Miracle Max pronounces Westley only "mostly" dead. Since he was fired by Prince Humperdinck and has held a grudge ever since, Max agrees to revive Westley so that Humperdinck will be humiliated when Westley steals away Buttercup.

14.   C. Six

The line is repeated six times in the film. In a 2012 interview, Patinkin said that strangers still come up to him every day and quote the line, and he loves the fact that he had the opportunity to be part of such an iconic film.

15.   B. Four white horses

An alternate ending for the film toyed with the idea of the grandson looking out of his window and seeing the characters on their four horses. But the filmmakers weren't sure the "real" world and the "book" world should collide, so they never filmed it.

QUESTIONS

16. True or false:

The Dread Pirate Roberts was a real pirate.

17. True or false:

Cary Elwes and Mandy Patinkin used stunt doubles for most of their sword fighting scenes.

18. True or false:

The film was wildly successful at the box office, becoming an instant classic.

19. Name the location:

The Cliffs of _____.

ANSWERS

16. True

Bartholomew Roberts, who was also known as Black Bart, sailed the Caribbean Sea in the 18th century. He is considered by some to be the most successful pirate who ever lived.

17. False

The duo underwent rigorous training for six months so they could perform their own sword fighting scenes. In the impressive fight on top of the cliff, the entire scene – save for one acrobatic backflip – is performed by the actors themselves, and took almost a week to shoot.

18. False

The movie only grossed $30.8 million, which was a tenth of what the year's biggest hit, Fatal Attraction, *brought in.* The Princess Bride *didn't discover its true popularity until VCRs became a household item.*

19. Insanity

The Cliffs of Insanity were created using a combination of painted sets and the actual Cliffs of Moher in County Clare, Ireland. Wallace Shawn (Vizzini) was so afraid of heights that André the Giant had to reassure him by whispering "Don't worry, I'll take care of you" as they ascended the cliff.

SHAUN OF THE DEAD

1. Who plays the title character in the 2004 "rom-zom-com" (romantic zombie comedy) *Shaun of the Dead?*

    A. Simon Pegg
    B. Rhys Darby
    C. Nick Frost
    D. Rafe Spall

2. Which director called *Shaun of the Dead* **"a masterpiece"?**

    A. Tim Burton
    B. J.J. Abrams
    C. Danny Boyle
    D. Quentin Tarantino

3. Where does Shaun work?

    A. Movie theater
    B. Grocery store
    C. Electronics store
    D. Pizza parlor

ANSWERS

1.   A. Simon Pegg

Pegg not only stars in the film – he co-wrote the script with director Edgar Wright. The two worked together on the British sitcom Spaced. *Incidentally, Nick Frost played Pegg's best friend in* Spaced, *and he also plays Shaun's best friend, Ed, in* Shaun of the Dead.

2.   D. Quentin Tarantino

Tarantino, known for his work on Pulp Fiction, Kill Bill, *and* Django Unchained, *said in a 2009 interview that* Shaun of the Dead *was one of the top 20 films made since the early 90s.*

3.   C. Electronics store

Shaun works at an electronics store called Foree Electronics. The name was the film-makers' nod to Ken Foree, an actor who starred in the 1978 film Dawn of the Dead.

QUESTIONS

4. What is the name of the pub that Shaun and Ed frequent?

    A. The Dog and Duck
    B. The Winchester
    C. The World's End
    D. The Duke

5. What song is playing on the jukebox in the pub after Liz breaks up with Shaun?

    A. "If You Leave Me Now"
    B. "You Oughta Know"
    C. "I Will Always Love You"
    D. "I Will Survive"

6. What is the name of Shaun and Ed's flatmate?

    A. David
    B. Phillip
    C. Danny
    D. Pete

7. What does Ed ask Shaun to buy him at the corner store?

    A. A can of soda
    B. A Cornetto ice cream cone
    C. Some beef jerky
    D. Dairy Milk chocolate

ANSWERS

4.   B. The Winchester

Shaun and Ed are so partial to the Winchester that they decide it will be the best place to wait out the zombie apocalypse. They also use a rifle they find behind the bar – a Winchester, of course – to fight off the horde. This is the same rifle used in 1968's Night of the Living Dead.

5.   A. *If You Leave Me Now*

Chicago's "If You Leave Me Now" was actually added to the scene after filming. During filming, the crew played Sinead O'Connor's "Nothing Compares 2 U." However, this song, written by Prince, was too expensive to be used for the movie.

6.   D. Pete

Pete is bitten by "some crackheads" on his way home and eventually transforms into a zombie. But first he shares a clue to the end of the movie, when he tells a lazy, unemployed Ed that he should "live in the shed."

7.   B. A Cornetto ice cream cone

Shaun of the Dead *is the first movie in what fans call "the Cornetto trilogy," all of which were written by Simon Pegg and Edgar Wright. In* Shaun of the Dead, *the cones come in red packages to symbolize blood and zombies. In 2007's* Hot Fuzz, *they are blue to symbolize the police. And in 2013's* The World's End, *they are green to symbolize aliens.*

QUESTIONS

8. What is the name of the zombie Shaun and Ed find in their garden?

    A. Mary
    B. Barbara
    C. Peggy
    D. Lucy

9. Why does Shaun tell Ed not to use "the zed word"?

    A. "Because it's offensive."
    B. "Because they don't exist."
    C. "Because it's ridiculous."
    D. "Because they might hear you."

10. Who plays Philip, Shaun's stepfather?

    A. Jim Broadbent
    B. Tom Wilkinson
    C. Ronald Pickup
    D. Bill Nighy

11. What are the names of Liz's friends who accompany the group to the pub?

    A. Dottie and David
    B. Dianne and David
    C. Yvonne and Danny
    D. Yvonne and David

ANSWERS

8.   **A. Mary**

In the opening montage, we see Mary before she is turned into a zombie, as a check-out girl in a grocery store. Shaun and Ed initially mistake her for a drunk girl when she shows up in their garden, but once they realize she is a zombie, they attempt to fight her off by flinging record albums at her.

9.   **C. "Because it's ridiculous."**

Shaun says that "it's ridiculous" to use "the zed word." This was the filmmaker's humorous reference to the fact that most zombie movies avoid using the word "zombie."

10.   **D. Bill Nighy**

Nighy says that Shaun of the Dead *"was one of the funniest scripts I'd read, ever." His role as Shaun's stepfather brings a moment of poignancy to the comedy, when Philip tells Shaun that he loves him before he dies and returns as a zombie.*

11.   **B. Dianne and David**

David is reluctant to head to the Winchester with the rest of the group, but relents when Dianne and Liz both decide to go. He is eventually dismembered by a zombie horde, leaving Dianne holding one of his legs. She runs out of the pub, swinging the leg and fighting through zombies. This is the last we see of her in the film. But the Shaun of the Dead *DVD bonus features reveal that she survived and went to live with her aunt.*

QUESTIONS

12. Which Queen song is playing on the jukebox when the group is fighting off the zombie in the pub?

    A. "Don't Stop Me Now"
    B. "We Are the Champions"
    C. "Another One Bites the Dust"
    D. "Bohemian Rhapsody"

13. After they settle in at the pub, who in the group is the first to die?

    A. David
    B. Dianne
    C. Barbara
    D. Ed

14. What happens to Ed at the end of the film?

    A. He gets a job
    B. He disappears
    C. Shaun shoots him
    D. He turns into a zombie

15. Which singer has a cameo as a zombie in the film?

    A. Rod Stewart
    B. Chris Martin
    C. Lily Allen
    D. Sting

ANSWERS

12.   A. Don't Stop Me Now

As the group attempts to keep the zombie at bay with pool cues, Shaun yells, "kill the Queen!" referring, of course, to the song on the jukebox. The next year, a Top Gear *viewer poll found "Don't Stop Me Now" to be the best road song.*

13.   C. Barbara

Sadly, Shaun's mother, Barbara, was bitten on the way to the pub. She kept it quiet so as not to worry anyone, but eventually she succumbs to the wound. When she reanimates as a zombie, a grief-stricken Shaun has no choice but to shoot her.

14.   D. He turns into a zombie

Ed becomes a zombie at the end of the film, but Shaun keeps him chained up in the shed where he can play video games all day – not unlike his life when he was human.

15.   B. Chris Martin

Chris Martin of Coldplay has a cameo as a zombie walking near the phone booth when Shaun and Liz are exiting the pub. He also plays himself at the end of the film, in a commercial for the "Zomb-Aid" charity.

QUESTIONS

16. Who is the British talk show host with a cameo at the end of the movie?

       A. Graham Norton
       B. James Corden
       C. Trisha Goddard
       D. Judy Finnigan

17. True or false:

The zombies in *Shaun of the Dead* move quickly, running after their prey and easily scaling obstacles.

18. True or false:

Simon Pegg and Nick Frost are friends in real life.

19. True or false:

When Shaun and the gang leave Liz's flat with their weapons, Shaun is the only one who ever actually attacks the zombies.

ANSWERS

16.   C. Trisha Goddard

On the fictional show, Goddard's guest is a woman who is in love with a zombie. The scene was filmed during breaks of her actual show, and the actors improvised their parts. Goddard also had a short-lived talk show in the U.S. that ran from 2012 to 2014.

17. False

When asked why the zombies in the film move so slowly, Simon Pegg said it was because "death is not an energy drink."

18. True

Pegg and Frost have been best friends for years. They based their movie friendship in Shaun of the Dead *on time they spent together as flatmates, when they were once so broke that they had to share a single bed.*

19. True

Simon Pegg was the only actor who was given a fake, padded bat. Everyone else was carrying real weapons that would've injured the actors playing the zombies if they'd been hit with them.

ZOOLANDER

1. Who directed the 2001 comedy *Zoolander*?

    A. Tom McGrath
    B. Ben Stiller
    C. John Hamburg
    D. Jay Roach

2. Who plays *Time* magazine journalist Matilda Jeffries?

    A. Christine Taylor
    B. Sienna Miller
    C. Carla Gugino
    D. Christina Applegate

3. Derek Zoolander's biggest rival is a model named Hansel. Which actor plays the role?

    A. Luke Wilson
    B. Will Ferrell
    C. Steve Carell
    D. Owen Wilson

ANSWERS

1.   B. Ben Stiller

Ben Stiller not only stars as the titular Derek Zoolander, but also directed the film and helped write the script.

2.   A. Christine Taylor

Christine Taylor and Ben Stiller have been married since May 13, 2000. They also worked together in Dodgeball: A True Underdog Story.

3.   D. Owen Wilson

Stiller has said that he wrote the part of Hansel specifically for Owen Wilson, and no one else was even considered for the part.

QUESTIONS

4. Who plays the part of Derek's coal-miner father, Larry, who is unimpressed with his son's modeling career?

        A. Jerry Stiller
        B. Christopher Lloyd
        C. Jon Voight
        D. Mel Brooks

5. What is the name of the "look" that Derek has been working on for years but has yet to unveil?

        A. Le Tigre
        B. Ferrari
        C. Blue Steel
        D. Magnum

6. Meekus, one of Derek's model roommates, is played by which *True Blood* actor?

        A. Alexander Skarsgard
        B. Stephen Moyer
        C. Nelsan Ellis
        D. Joe Manganiello

7. What sort of drink do Derek's roommates suggest will help him feel better after his award loss to Hansel?

        A. Whiskey
        B. Orange Mocha Frappuccinos
        C. Strawberry milkshakes
        D. Sour appletinis

ANSWERS

4.   C. Jon Voight

Although Derek's father in the film is played by Jon Voight, Stiller's actual father, Jerry Stiller, also appears in the movie as Derek's agent, Maury Ballstein. Stiller's mother, sister, and brother-in-law all have cameos, as well. The movie was quite the family affair!

5.   D. Magnum

Stiller has said that the idea for Derek Zoolander's "model looks" – which, hilariously, all look exactly the same – came about from his wife's teasing him about the way he looks at himself in the mirror when he combs his hair.

6.   A. Alexander Skarsgard

Already a star in his native Sweden, actor Alexander Skarsgard made his American film debut in Zoolander.

7.   B. Orange Mocha Frappuccinos

Although the idea of an orange mocha Frappuccino was made up for the movie, Starbucks sold the drink for a limited time in the U.S. in 2007, and began selling them in Japan in 2015.

QUESTIONS

8. What is the name of the cemetery where the models are buried after their "freak gasoline fight accident"?

    A. Saint Anthony
    B. Saint Ignatius
    C. Saint Adonis
    D. Saint Augustine

9. Will Ferrell's character, Mugatu, was modeled after a character from an episode of what show?

    A. *Star Trek*
    B. *The X-Files*
    C. *Friends*
    D. *The Simpsons*

10. Who is the judge for Derek and Hansel's walk-off?

    A. Fabio
    B. Tyson Beckford
    C. Victoria Beckham
    D. David Bowie

11. Which direction is Derek unable to turn?

    A. Right
    B. In a circle
    C. Left
    D. He can only go in a straight line

ANSWERS

8. C. Saint Adonis

Adonis was not, in fact, a saint, but rather a figure of Greek mythology. According to the story, both Aphrodite and Persephone fell in love with him because of his great beauty. Obviously "Saint Adonis Cemetery" was the perfect final resting place for models.

9. A. *Star Trek*

In the second season of the original Star Trek *series, the episode "A Private Little War" introduced a white-fur-covered creature called the Mugato. Both William Shatner and DeForest Kelley pronounced it as "Mugatu" throughout the episode, and consequently, it is often misspelled.*

10. D. David Bowie

Ben Stiller wrote the "walk-off" scene specifically with David Bowie in mind, not knowing if the singer would actually agree to appear in the film.

11. C. Left

After Derek loses the walk-off to Hansel, he confesses to Matilda, "I'm not an ambi-turner. It's a problem I've had since I was a baby. I can't turn left."

QUESTIONS

12. How does Derek spell "day"?

    A. Daiye
    B. Daye
    C. Daie
    D. Day

13. Who plays hand model J.P. Prewitt?

    A. Christian Slater
    B. David Duchovny
    C. Bryan Cranston
    D. Kevin Spacey

14. Derek is brainwashed by Mugatu to try to force him to assassinate the prime minister of which country?

    A. Malaysia
    B. Indonesia
    C. Micronesia
    D. Japan

15. Which celebrity does NOT have a cameo in the film?

    A. Donald Trump
    B. Winona Ryder
    C. Natalie Portman
    D. Anne Hathaway

ANSWERS

12. A. Daiye

Derek doesn't realize that he's been at the spa for an entire week. When Matilda tells him that she's been trying to get a hold of him for that long, he thinks it's impossible, because "I was at a day spa. Day. D-A-I-Y-E."

13. B. David Duchovny

J.P. Prewitt is a retired hand model who believes that the fashion industry is the mastermind behind political assassinations. This "conspiracy theorist" character is not unlike Duchovny's role as Fox Mulder on The X-Files.

14. A. Malaysia

Because of the jokes about the country and the assassination story, Zoolander *has been banned in Malaysia. It joins an extensive list of films that have been banned at one time or another in the country, including* The King and I, Jaws, Schindler's List, *and* Saving Private Ryan.

15. D. Anne Hathaway

Zoolander *has quite a few celebrity cameos, including appearances from Christian Slater, Gwen Stefani, James Marsden, Billy Zane, and hairstylist Frederic Fekkai. Vince Vaughn has a small role as Derek's brother, Luke Zoolander, but he has no lines in the movie.*

QUESTIONS

16. True or false:

Owen Wilson grew out his hair to shoulder length for the movie.

17. Finish the name:

The Derek Zoolander Center for Kids Who Can't Read Good and _____.

18. Finish the commercial line:

Moisture is the essence of wetness, and wetness is the essence of _____.

ANSWERS

16. False

Wilson was filming the military drama Behind Enemy Lines *at the same time, which required him to keep his hair short. His flowing locks in* Zoolander *were courtesy of a wig. Will Ferrell's hair for Mugatu, however, was his own hair dyed platinum blond.*

17. Who Wanna Learn to Do Other Stuff Good, Too

This is where Derek teaches kids that "there's more to life than being really, really ridiculously good-looking."

18. Beauty

The commercial for Aveda comes on in the bar after Derek has spent a day working in a coal mine with his father and brothers. His father laments the fact that his son is a model, saying he's glad his mother didn't live to see him as a mermaid. To which Derek retorts, "mer-man!"

BIG

1. In the heartwarming 1988 comedy *Big,* a 12-year-old boy's wish to be "big" comes true. Who directed the film?

    A. Garry Marshall
    B. Nora Ephron
    C. Penny Marshall
    D. Jon Turteltaub

2. Which popular actor plays the part of older Josh?

    A. Brad Pitt
    B. Tom Hanks
    C. Tom Cruise
    D. Johnny Depp

3. What is the name of the magical fortune-telling machine Josh finds at the amusement park?

    A. Zoltar
    B. Zumba
    C. Zandar
    D. The Oracle

ANSWERS

1.   C. Penny Marshall

With Big, *Penny Marshall became first female director to direct a movie that grossed more than $100 million at the box office.*

2.   B. Tom Hanks

Tom Hanks was praised for his portrayal of a child who is trapped in the body of an adult. He won a Golden Globe for his performance, and was nominated for a Best Actor Oscar.

3.   A. Zoltar

The scene at the beginning of the movie where Josh first finds the Zoltar machine was filmed at Ross Dock Picnic Area on the Hudson River in Fort Lee, New Jersey. The scene when he finds the machine again at the end was filmed at Rye Playland Amusement Park in Westchester County, New York, which has been in operation since 1928.

QUESTIONS

4. What is unusual about the machine Josh uses to make his wish?

    A. A sign on it says "out of order"
    B. The instructions are written in Russian
    C. The mechanical face inside looks just like Josh
    D. It is unplugged

5. When Josh first wakes up to find himself in an older body, he attempts to convince his frightened mother that he is still her son. Which proof does he NOT offer?

    A. His birthday
    B. The location of his birthmark
    C. His favorite TV show
    D. The grade he got on his history test

6. What is the name of Josh's best friend?

    A. Timmy
    B. Billy
    C. Tommy
    D. Bobby

7. What is the name of the hotel where Josh stays in New York?

    A. St. Regis
    B. Park Hotel
    C. Hotel Broadway
    D. St. James

ANSWERS

4.   D. It is unplugged

After Josh is barred from riding a roller coaster because he isn't tall enough, he finds the wishing machine and knows just what to wish for. The machine tells him his wish will be granted, but then he notices that the mysterious machine is unplugged.

5.   C. His favorite TV show

Josh tells his mom about his birthday, a birthmark behind his knee, and the B he got on his history test, but none of it convinces her. Incidentally, in a "movie goof" moment, older Josh tells his mom that his birthday is in November. However, we later see a milk carton with a "missing" photo of Josh, where his birthday is listed as being in January. No wonder his mom didn't believe him!

6.   B. Billy

Older Josh manages to convince Billy that he is who he says he is by singing the "shimmy shimmy cocoa pop" song the two of them made up. Tom Hanks has stated that the silly song was inspired by a song his son learned at summer camp.

7.   D. St. James

The St. James is a real hotel in New York City, which was brave enough to lend its name and location for the "seedy" hotel Josh encounters. Fortunately for travelers, the actual St. James is nothing like its unsavory movie counterpart.

QUESTIONS

8. Josh is able to land a job at the MacMillan Toy Company. Which actor plays the head of the company?

    A. Gene Hackman
    B. Jon Voight
    C. Robert Loggia
    D. Frank Langella

9. Who plays the part of Susan, Josh's co-worker and later love interest?

    A. Elizabeth Perkins
    B. Julianne Moore
    C. Mary-Louise Parker
    D. Marisa Tomei

10. How much does Josh receive in his first paycheck?

    A. $214
    B. $187
    C. $164
    D. $253

11. What position is Josh eventually promoted to within the company?

    A. Vice president
    B. Senior toy tester
    C. Executive assistant
    D. Head of manufacturing

ANSWERS

8.   C. Robert Loggia

Robert Loggia plays the CEO of the MacMillan Toy Company. His character was based on Peter Harris, who was the CEO of toy company FAO Schwarz at the time.

9.   A. Elizabeth Perkins

Originally, the filmmakers wanted Debra Winger in the role of Susan, but she happened to be pregnant at the time of shooting. Winger herself recommended Perkins for the part.

10.   B. $187

We know the amount of Josh's first paycheck, because as soon as he sees it he excitedly exclaims, "187 dollars!" This is a lot of money for a 12-year-old, but his office colleagues are not nearly so impressed with their own paychecks.

11.   A. Vice president

MacMillan is so impressed with Josh's uncanny ability to understand what kids like that he promotes him to vice president. He doesn't realize, of course, that Josh is still a kid himself.

QUESTIONS

12. What is the name of Susan's boyfriend, who dislikes Josh and is jealous of his quick climb in the company?

    A. Robert
    B. Scotty
    C. Paul
    D. David

13. Where was the famous "giant piano" scene filmed?

    A. On a Hollywood sound stage
    B. At Toys R Us
    C. In a New York warehouse
    D. At FAO Schwarz

14. What does Josh wear to the company party?

    A. A baseball jersey
    B. A three-piece suit
    C. A white tuxedo
    D. A superhero t-shirt

15. Once Josh is promoted, he is able to rent a huge apartment. What does he NOT buy for his new digs?

    A. Trampoline
    B. Waterbed
    C. Pinball machine
    D. Inflatable dinosaur

ANSWERS

12.   C. Paul

Paul is played by actor John Heard, who went on to appear in the wildly popular Home Alone *movies as dad Peter McCallister.*

13.   D. At FAO Schwarz

The famous scene was filmed at the now-closed FAO Schwarz flagship store on Fifth Avenue. Robert Loggia has said that doubles were on hand to play the giant piano in case he and Tom Hanks weren't able to do it. This made them even more determined to perform the song themselves.

14.   C. A white tuxedo

Not only is the tuxedo Josh wears white, but it also has sparkling, glittering accents. Needless to say, he stands out from his business-attired coworkers at the party.

15.   B. Waterbed

Josh's apartment is every 12-year-old's dream, complete with a trampoline, a soda machine that dispenses free soda, a pinball machine, and a basketball court. Susan is a bit perplexed when their "sleepover" concludes with Josh in the top bunk of his bunkbed, and her on the bottom.

QUESTIONS

16. When Josh tells Susan that he's keeping a secret, what does she first think he's trying to tell her?

    A. He's married
    B. He has kids
    C. He's divorced
    D. He's broke

17. True or false:

The credits tell us that Josh's baby sister, Rachel, was played by Mary-Kate and Ashley Olsen.

18. True or false:

A musical version of *Big* was created for Broadway in the 90s.

ANSWERS

16.   A. He's married

Susan first assumes that Josh is trying to tell her that he's married. He finally confesses to her that he's just a kid, but she misunderstands and takes it to mean that he's insecure and afraid of commitment.

17. False

The name of the child (or children) who played Rachel was not in the credits, and, in fact, remains unknown.

18. True

The musical opened on April 28, 1996 at the Shubert Theater, but only ran for 193 performances, closing on October 13, 1996. Still, it was nominated for five Tony Awards, including Best Actress, Supporting Actor, Book, Score, and Choreography.

HARRY POTTER

1. Which of these directors did NOT direct at least one installment of the *Harry Potter* series?

    A. Alfonso Cuaron
    B. Chris Columbus
    C. Mike Newell
    D. Robert Zemeckis

2. Who was the first actor to be cast for the films?

    A. Daniel Radcliffe, as Harry Potter
    B. Robbie Coltrane, as Rubeus Hagrid
    C. Matthew Lewis, as Neville Longbottom
    D. John Hurt, as Mr. Ollivander

3. At the time that the first movie, *Harry Potter and the Sorcerer's Stone*, was being filmed, how many of J.K. Rowling's novels had been completed?

    A. 3
    B. 4
    C. 5
    D. 6

ANSWERS

1.   D. Robert Zemeckis

Chris Columbus directed the first two films, Harry Potter and the Sorcerer's Stone *and* Harry Potter and the Chamber of Secrets; *Alfonso Cuaron directed* Harry Potter and the Prisoner of Azkaban; *Mike Newell directed* Harry Potter and the Goblet of Fire; *and David Yates directed the final four films:* Harry Potter and the Order of the Phoenix, Harry Potter and the Half-Blood Prince, *and* Harry Potter and the Deathly Hollows, *parts I and II.*

2.   B. Robbie Coltrane, as Rubeus Hagrid

J.K. Rowling specifically chose Robbie Coltrane for the role of Hagrid, and he was the first to be cast. Throughout the years of filming, Coltrane and Rowling became good friends, and Coltrane has stated that he believes Rowling deserves all the wealth and fame she has because of "all the millions of children she's encouraged to read."

3.   B. 4

Four of the books had been written when production for the first film began. The producers first considered making all of the movies animated CGI, so as not to worry about the quickly changing appearance of the child actors. But since J.K. Rowling didn't like this idea, they instead decided to simply film all the movies back-to-back as quickly as possible.

QUESTIONS

4. Which train platform is used to get to the magical Hogwarts Express?

    A. 5 ¾
    B. 9 ½
    C. 9 ¾
    D. 3 ¾

5. Who plays Professor Albus Dumbledore in the first two *Harry Potter* films?

    A. Richard Harris
    B. Peter O'Toole
    C. Ian McKellen
    D. Anthony Hopkins

6. What is the name of the alchemist who is said to have created the "Sorcerer's Stone" in the first film?

    A. Albertus Magnus
    B. Johann Faust
    C. Nicolas Flamel
    D. Benedictus Figulus

7. Which actress plays Hermione Granger?

    A. Emma Watson
    B. Bonnie Wright
    C. Emily Dale
    D. Evanna Lynch

ANSWERS

4.   C. 9 ¾

There is now an actual "Platform 9 ¾" at King's Cross Station in London, where one quarter of a luggage cart has been affixed to the wall. Fans can get a picture of themselves "disappearing" into the platform.

5.   A. Richard Harris

Richard Harris took on the part of Dumbledore after the original actor cast for the part, Patrick McGoohan, had health issues. Sadly, Harris himself succumbed to Hodgkin's lymphoma in 2002 and was replaced by Michael Gambon.

6.   C. Nicolas Flamel

Nicolas Flamel was a French scribe and manuscript seller born around 1330, who died in 1418. It wasn't until the seventeenth century that he was rumored to be an alchemist, and there is no actual evidence that he dabbled in alchemy. But this hasn't stopped his name from popping up as a plot device in many stories, such as the Indiana Jones *novels and Dan Brown's* The Da Vinci Code.

7.   A. Emma Watson

When the production team held a casting call at her elementary school, Emma Watson had no interest in auditioning. It was only after a teacher encouraged her that she agreed to audition. She was the last girl in her school to do so.

QUESTIONS

8. Which composer wrote the main theme for the *Harry Potter* movies?

    A. James Horner
    B. James Newton Howard
    C. Hans Zimmer
    D. John Williams

9. Daniel Radcliffe, who plays Harry Potter, appeared in which film before starring in the *Harry Potter* series?

    A. Spy Kids
    B. Gosford Park
    C. The Tailor of Panama
    D. The Others

10. How tall is the unusually large Hagrid?

    A. 8 feet 6 inches
    B. 7 feet 5 inches
    C. 8 feet 2 inches
    D. 7 feet 10 inches

11. What is the name of Harry's owl?

    A. Horus
    B. Hedwig
    C. Crookshanks
    D. Errol

ANSWERS

8.   D. John Williams

Prolific composer John Williams wrote the entire score for the first three Harry Potter *films. And although the later films were scored by Patrick Doyle, Nicholas Hooper, and Alexandre Desplat, Williams' famous theme, called "Hedwig's Theme," is used in all eight movies.*

9.   C. The Tailor of Panama

Radcliffe played Mark Pendel in The Tailor of Panama, *working alongside Pierce Brosnan and Geoffrey Rush. Even a decade after appearing in the film, Radcliffe had never seen it, preferring to avoid watching his own performance. He also tries not to read any articles or reviews about himself or his films.*

10.   A. 8 feet 6 inches

Robbie Coltraine, who plays Hagrid, is 6'1". His body double for Hagrid was a former rugby player named Martin Bayfield, who stands at an impressive (although not quite Hagrid-sized) 6'10".

11.   B. Hedwig

Hedwig was played by a total of seven snowy owls, which were shipped over to the U.K. from Massachusetts. Because of their "snow white" appearance, male owls were used for filming, even though Hedwig is described as a female.

QUESTIONS

12. Why is Rupert Grint, who plays Ron, still reluctant to watch *Harry Potter and the Chamber of Secrets?*

    A. He is afraid of snakes
    B. He was unhappy with his acting performance
    C. He is afraid of spiders
    D. It was his least favorite book

13. Who plays the role of prickly potions master Severus Snape?

    A. Richard Griffiths
    B. Jason Isaacs
    C. Tom Felton
    D. Alan Rickman

14. Approximately how many wands did Daniel Radcliffe go through during the filming of the *Harry Potter* movies?

    A. 35
    B. 50
    C. 70
    D. 85

15. Which actor plays Harry's rival, Draco Malfoy?

    A. Tom Felton
    B. Jason Isaacs
    C. Timothy Spall
    D. Robert Pattinson

ANSWERS

12. C. He is afraid of spiders

Grint reportedly suffers from a severe case of arachnophobia, and has refused to watch the film because of the scene with Aragog, a giant spider with many sons and daughters. Grint didn't need to rely on acting talent to display the fright seen in the film – he was genuinely terrified!

13. D. Alan Rickman

Rickman was another actor hand-picked by J.K. Rowling for a specific part. After his death in January 2016, Rowling revealed that she told him the end of Snape's story, even before she had finished the books, so he would understand the character's motivations.

14. C. 70

Radcliffe liked to use his prop wands as drumsticks, so he often broke them. He also went through 160 pairs of glasses. More than 3000 wands were used in total for all the characters throughout the series. All the wands were made on-site, and no two were alike.

15. A. Tom Felton

When he was cast for the part of Malfoy, Felton hadn't read any of the Harry Potter books. His naturally light brown hair had to be dyed blond to stay true to the character.

QUESTIONS

16. The evil Lord Voldemort, also known as He Who Must Not Be Named, is played by which actor?

      A. Colin Firth
      B. Ralph Fiennes
      C. Paul Bettany
      D. Sean Bean

17. What does the name "Voldemort" mean?

      A. Nameless One
      B. Death of Good
      C. Flight of Death
      D. Story End

18. True or false:

Daniel Radcliffe's blue eyes are consistent with Harry's blue eyes in the books.

19. True or false:

Actress Evanna Lynch, who plays Luna Lovegood, actually helped design her character's eccentric look.

20. True or false:

None of the films in the *Harry Potter* series ever won an Oscar.

ANSWERS

16.   B. Ralph Fiennes

Fiennes has said that he tried to imagine Voldemort as an orphan who was never loved and was always isolated, which led to his evil behavior. He felt most like his character when he donned Voldemort's long, black robes, and even inadvertently caused small children who visited the set to burst into tears at his fearsome appearance.

17.   C. Flight of Death

In French, "Voldemort" means "flight of death" or, perhaps more appropriate, "steal/cheat death." Voldemort created the "Horcruxes" in a futile attempt to cheat death.

18. False

In the books, Harry's eyes are green. Radcliffe was originally fitted with green contacts to stay true to the character's appearance in the books, but he had a bad reaction to them. J.K. Rowling decided it would be acceptable if "movie Harry" had blue eyes.

19. True

Lynch wore many of her own pieces of clothing and jewelry during the films. She even handmade the radish earrings Luna wears in Harry Potter and the Order of the Phoenix.

20. True

Although the series was nominated for a total of 12 Oscars, none of the films ever won.

MEAN GIRLS

1. Who wrote the screenplay for the 2004 comedy *Mean Girls?*

    A. Kay Cannon
    B. Amy Poehler
    C. Amy Heckerling
    D. Tina Fey

2. Who plays the part of the new girl at school, Cady Heron?

    A. Megan Fox
    B. Kat Dennings
    C. Lindsay Lohan
    D. Amanda Bynes

3. *Mean Girls* marks the feature film debut of which popular actress?

    A. Amanda Seyfried
    B. Rachel McAdams
    C. Anna Kendrick
    D. Kaley Cuoco

ANSWERS

1.   D. Tina Fey

Mean Girls marked Fey's feature film screenwriting debut. The movie was based on the book "Queen Bees and Wannabes" by Rosalind Wiseman, which is a non-fiction self-help guide for parents. Fey agreed to adapt the book into a screenplay before she even realized it was non-fiction.

2.   C. Lindsay Lohan

Lohan was originally interested in the part of Regina George, the leader of the "mean girl" clique. But she was afraid that fans would assume her true personality was like the character's, so she opted for a "nice girl" instead.

3.   A. Amanda Seyfried

After appearing on the soap operas As the World Turns *and* All My Children, *Seyfried landed the role of Karen in* Mean Girls. *She has since gone on to star in movies like* Mamma Mia!, Dear John, *and* Les Miserables, *and she spent five seasons playing "Sarah Henrickson" on HBO's* Big Love.

QUESTIONS

4. Where did Cady live before moving to the U.S.?

    A. China
    B. Paris
    C. Africa
    D. Australia

5. During her first week at her new school, Cady meets Regina, Gretchen, and Karen, who are known as what?

    A. The Shallows
    B. The Plastics
    C. The Mean Girls
    D. The Rich Girls

6. Which of these is NOT one of Regina's rules for her group?

    A. You can't wear a tank top two days in a row
    B. You can only wear your hair in a ponytail one day a week
    C. You can only wear jeans on Fridays
    D. Your shoes and bag should always match

7. Which actress plays Regina's mom, Mrs. George?

    A. Amy Poehler
    B. Tina Fey
    C. Ana Gasteyer
    D. Heather Graham

ANSWERS

4.   C. Africa

Although the exact country is never specified, Cady moved to the U.S. from somewhere in Africa, where her parents were research zoologists. Since she was home-schooled her whole life, she is unfamiliar with the dynamics of high school life.

5.   B. The Plastics

The clique is known around school as "The Plastics," although the three girls never actually refer to themselves as such.

6.   D. Your shoes and bag should always match

In addition to their "fashion" rules, the Plastics closely monitor their social lives, as well. They have to vote before adding anyone (like Cady) to their lunch group, and they decree that ex-boyfriends are off limits to friends.

7.   A. Amy Poehler

Poehler hilariously portrays Mrs. George as a woman who is desperately trying to hang on to her teenage years. This works out especially well since Poehler is only seven years older than her movie daughter, Rachel McAdams!

QUESTIONS

8. What is the name of the guy Cady likes?

    A. Damian
    B. Kevin
    C. Aaron
    D. Shane

9. What color does Regina's clique wear on Wednesdays?

    A. Blue
    B. Pink
    C. Green
    D. Yellow

10. What does Cady trick Regina into eating in an effort to sabotage her weight-loss efforts?

    A. Chocolate
    B. Cheese
    C. Danish pastries
    D. Energy bars

11. Where does Regina attempt to buy a prom dress?

    A. 1-3-5
    B. Barney's
    C. Nordstrom
    D. Sears

ANSWERS

8.   C. Aaron

Cady falls for Regina's ex-boyfriend, Aaron. To gain his attention, she pretends to be confused by math problems so he'll tutor her, even though she excels at math.

9.   B. Pink

"On Wednesdays, we wear pink," is what Karen tells Cady when the Plastics first invite her to their lunch table. Incidentally, a total of 21 pink tops were worn by the girls throughout the film.

10.   D. Energy bars

Cady gives Regina "Kalteen" bars, which she tells her are Swedish nutrition bars that will "burn all your carbs." In reality, Cady's mom used to give them to kids in Africa to help them gain weight.

11.   A. 1-3-5

As the name suggests, the store sells only sizes 1, 3, and 5. But after eating so many Kalteen bars, Regina can't fit into any of the dresses, so the snooty clerk suggests she "try Sears."

QUESTIONS

12. What does a girl at school buy just because she saw Cady wearing them?

        A. A t-shirt and a headband
        B. Shorts and clogs
        C. Army pants and flip flops
        D. A skirt and a baseball cap

13. What did Gretchen's dad invent that led to her family's wealth?

        A. Velcro
        B. Toaster Strudel
        C. Microwave popcorn
        D. Hair scrunchies

14. Which girl adds herself to the mean-spirited, gossipy "Burn Book"?

        A. Cady
        B. Gretchen
        C. Karen
        D. Regina

15. What is Cady's answer to the question that wins the Mathlympics?

        A. -1
        B. Pi squared
        C. The limit does not exist
        D. 42

ANSWERS

12.   C. Army pants and flip flops

Once Cady works her way into the Plastics clique, she becomes one of the "popular" girls. So even something as mundane as army pants and flip flops is a coveted ensemble.

13.   B. Toaster Strudel

Gretchen, played by Lacey Chabert of Party of Five fame, comes from a wealthy family thanks to her father's Toaster Strudel discovery.

14.   D. Regina

When Regina discovers that Cady has been attempting to sabotage her diet and pursuing her ex-boyfriend, she retaliates by spreading the Burn Book rumors throughout the whole school. But first she adds her own name, so it will look like she had no part in writing the book.

15.   C. The limit does not exist

After her opponent answers incorrectly, Cady is given the chance to "find the limit of this equation." It takes some time, and some musing about "limits" in her own life, but she eventually recalls a lesson in math class that jogs her memory.

QUESTIONS

16. Who are the two real friends Cady makes at her school?

    A. Janis and Damian
    B. Jennifer and Danny
    C. Jennifer and Damian
    D. Janis and Daniel

17. What does "Regina" mean in Latin?

    A. Leader
    B. Queen
    C. Princess
    D. Ruler

18. Finish the quote:

"I'm not like a regular mom, I'm _____."

ANSWERS

16.   A. Janis and Damian

The character of Janis was named in honor of Janis Ian, the first ever musical guest to appear on Saturday Night Live. *Damian was named after* TV Guide *writer Damian Holbrook, who has been friends with Tina Fey since the two were teenagers.*

17.   B. Queen

In the book the movie is based on, Queen Bees and Wannabes, *the "Queen Bee" is said to be the most popular girl in school.*

18. A Cool Mom

Mrs. George attempts to fit in with her teenager's friends by serving them non-alcoholic drinks for "happy hour." She also offers them alcohol if they want it "because if you're going to drink I'd rather you do it in the house." When she tries to get Regina to agree that she's a "cool mom," Regina begs her to "please stop talking."

REAL
GENIUS

1. In what year was the film *Real Genius* released?

     A.1984
     B. 1985
     C. 1986
     D. 1987

2. At which school does the story take place?

     A. Los Angeles Tech
     B. Southern California University
     C. Pacific Tech
     D. California College

3. Who plays Chris Knight, "one of the ten finest minds in the country"?

     A. John Cusack
     B. Matthew Broderick
     C. Val Kilmer
     D. Josh Brolin

ANSWERS

1.   B. 1985

Interestingly, the 1985 film was the first movie to be promoted via internet. The crew held a promotional press conference through CompuServe, where entertainment writers could submit questions digitally. Commonplace these days, but quite a big deal for 1985!

2.   C. Pacific Tech

In the movie, the school is called Pacific Tech, and it was filmed at Pomona College and Occidental College. But the story was very loosely based on actual events which occurred at the California Institute of Technology in Pasadena, California.

3.   C. Val Kilmer

Kilmer recalls that when he auditioned for the part, he tried to behave in a way his character would behave. So when producer Brian Grazer introduced himself, Kilmer said, "I'm sorry, you look like you're 12 years old. I like to work with men." Just like something smart-alecky Chris Knight would say!

QUESTIONS

4. What does Chris' shirt say when we first see him?

    A. I (heart) New York
    B. Harley Davidson
    C. Genius at Work
    D. I (heart) Toxic Waste

5. What is the name of the top secret CIA project in need of a powerful laser?

    A. Crossbow
    B. Laser Eye
    C. Crosshair
    D. Saber

6. How old is genius Mitch Taylor, who is admitted to the university after his high school science fair?

    A. 13
    B. 14
    C. 15
    D. 16

7. What is unusual about the ice in the "smart people on ice" skating scene?

    A. It is rainbow colored
    B. It turns directly from a solid to a gas
    C. It isn't cold
    D. It's made of salt water

ANSWERS

4.   D. I (heart) Toxic Waste

Chris expresses his apparent love of toxic waste in the first t-shirt he wears in the film. Other shirts include one with a picture of Roy Rogers, and messages such as "Surf Nicaragua," "International Order for Gorillas," and "The Monkees."

5.   A. Crossbow

Director Martha Coolidge strove for accuracy with the science in the film, but the deadly "Crossbow" project was one instance that she decided to create something impossible. "We didn't want to inspire any lethal tinkering," she explains.

6.   C. 15

Physics professor Dr. Hathaway mentions that the youngest student to ever be admitted was 12 years old. But he "cracked under the pressure." This was supposedly a reference to an actual Caltech student.

7.   B. It turns directly from a solid to a gas

The "skating rink" is easy to clean up, since it eventually vaporizes. To create the ice for the scene, the filmmakers had to use thousands of feet of tubing connected to refrigeration units under the floor.

QUESTIONS

8. What is the name of the girl who befriends Mitch?

    A. Jordan
    B. Janet
    C. Janice
    D. Jennifer

9. What is the name of the student who acts as Dr. Hathaway's right-hand man?

    A. Larry
    B. Carter
    C. Milton
    D. Kent

10. Who keeps disappearing into Chris and Mitch's dorm closet?

    A. Sherry Nugil
    B. Lazlo Hollyfeld
    C. David Decker
    D. Martin Gunderson

11. How many megawatts does Dr. Hathaway keep saying he wants "by mid-May"?

    A. 3
    B. 4
    C. 5
    D. 6

ANSWERS

8.   A. Jordan

In the film, the quirky Jordan knits Mitch a sweater overnight. The character was based on an actual Caltech student named Phyllis Rostykus, who first met with the producers and director of the film wearing a sweater she'd knitted the night before.

9.   D. Kent

Kent was played by actor Robert Prescott, who was already known for playing another "jerk," Cole Whittier, opposite Tom Hanks in Bachelor Party.

10.   B. Lazlo Hollyfeld

Chris tells Mitch that Hollyfeld was the number one student in the '70s, but the pressure got to him and he withdrew into seclusion. Mitch eventually figures out how to open the secret panel in the closet and finds Hollyfeld's hideout in the steam tunnels.

11.   C. 5

Dr. Hathaway needs the laser to be powerful enough for the secret CIA weapon to work. Incidentally, Albert Einstein, whose picture adorns Chris' dorm wall, won a Nobel Prize in 1921 for his Photon Theory, in which he first proposed the idea of a laser.

QUESTIONS

12. How does Mitch get back at Kent after Kent records Mitch's tearful phone call home and plays it for everyone to hear in the cafeteria?

    A. Destroys Kent's work in the lab
    B. Steals all his notes before a test
    C. Cuts off the hot water to the bathroom
    D. Dismantles his car and moves it into his dorm room

13. Lazlo Hollyfeld spends much of his time generating entries for the Frito-Lay Sweepstakes. What percentage of the prizes does he expect to win?

    A. 32.6%
    B. 29.1%
    C. 30.5%
    D. 33.3%

14. How does the group convince Kent that Jesus is talking to him?

    A. They hide a speaker in his room
    B. They implant a transceiver in his braces
    C. They glue a tiny radio to his glasses
    D. They hypnotize him

15. Who finally realizes the horrible potential of Chris and Mitch's laser?

    A. Mitch
    B. Jordan
    C. Chris
    D. Lazlo

ANSWERS

12.   D. Dismantles his car and moves it into his dorm room

Chris tells Mitch that it is a "moral imperative" to get even with Kent, so they sneak out to the parking lot and begin dismantling Kent's car. When Kent later returns to his dorm room, the entire car is sitting inside.

13.   A. 32.6

Hollyfeld takes advantage of the "enter as often as you want" stipulation and enters the sweepstakes more than a million times. He expects to win 32.6% of the prizes, "including the car." He ends up winning 31.8%, including an RV.

14.   B. They implant a transceiver in his braces

After snaking a tube under his dorm room door, the group pumps knockout gas into Kent's room and implants the transceiver while he's asleep. Jordan explains that his braces will act as an antenna, making his whole head a speaker.

15.   D. Lazlo

Feeling triumphant after their successful laser test, the group goes out to celebrate. Their carefree dinner is interrupted when Lazlo shows up and questions why Dr. Hathaway would want such a powerful laser. They rush back to the lab, only to discover that their project has been stolen.

QUESTIONS

16. How long did it take to pop all the popcorn in the final scenes?

        A. Three days
        B. Three weeks
        C. Three months
        D. It wasn't actually popcorn

17. True or false:

Many of the crazy pranks in the film were based on real college pranks.

18. True or false:

The professor who ends up with a classroom full of tape recorders was played by a real university professor.

ANSWERS

16.   C. Three months

It took three months to pop all of the popcorn used for the "popcorn house" scene. Producer Brian Grazer said the set "was one enormous popcorn popper," but the film crew still wasn't able to make enough. So the Lapidus Popcorn Company in Los Angeles popped an additional 90,000 cubic feet. In the end, the house was filled with enough popcorn to feed 720,000 moviegoers.

17. True

Many of the antics in the film were based on actual pranks that have occurred in schools such as Cambridge University in England, the Massachusetts Institute of Technology, and, of course, Caltech. In fact, the scene where the students have converted their dorm into a skating rink was based on an old practice at Caltech called "alley surfing," where the cement floor of a dorm basement would be covered with a layer of soapy water so students could "skate" over it.

18. True

Martin Gunderson was a physics professor from the University of Southern California. In addition to playing the role of the math professor, he was the technical advisor on the film, having worked on an infrared laser project at the Los Alamos National Laboratory.

THE
SANDLOT

1. In what year does the 1993 film *The Sandlot* take place?

    A. 1959
    B. 1960
    C. 1962
    D. 1965

2. Who plays Scotty's stepdad, Bill?

    A. Denis Leary
    B. Judge Reinhold
    C. Daniel Stern
    D. Kevin Costner

3. Which actress plays Scotty's mom?

    A. Catherine Hicks
    B. Karen Allen
    C. Melanie Griffith
    D. Holly Hunter

ANSWERS

1.   C. 1962

The narrator, an older Scotty Smalls, tells us that the story takes place in the summer of 1962, the year that the stolen base record was broken by Los Angeles Dodger Maury Wills.

2.   A. Denis Leary

In the film, Leary's character loves the New York Yankees and has a prized baseball signed by Babe Ruth. But in reality, Leary is a die-hard Boston Red Sox fan and hates the Yankees!

3.   B. Karen Allen

Karen Allen is best known for her role as Indiana Jones' love interest, Marion Ravenwood, in Raiders of the Lost Ark. *She has also starred in movies like* Starman, Scrooged, *and* The Perfect Storm.

QUESTIONS

4. What does Scotty say when he first hears Ham talking about "The Great Bambino"?

      A. "Best player ever!"
      B. "What's a bambino?"
      C. "He's great!"
      D. "Who's that?"

5. Benny tells Scotty he should throw a baseball how?

      A. Like tossing a stick
      B. Like throwing a paper on a paper route
      C. Like throwing a Frisbee
      D. Like casting a fishing rod

6. What do the boys say when Scotty first catches a glimpse of "the beast" and he asks what it is?

      A. Monster!
      B. A giant dog!
      C. Camp out!
      D. Don't ask!

7. What is the name of the lifeguard at the pool?

      A. Wendy Peffercorn
      B. Jenny Peterson
      C. Jenny Peffercorn
      D. Amanda Peterson

ANSWERS

4.   D. Who's that?

Scotty sees Ham's impression of "The Great Bambino," and asks, "Who's that?" This stuns the group of baseball-loving boys. Later, Scotty starts a list entitled "Baseball Stuff to Remember" with "The Great Bambino" at the top of the list.

5.   B. Like throwing a paper on a paper route

Even after asking his stepdad to teach him how to throw, Scotty is terrible at the game. It's only after Benny tells him to visualize throwing the ball like a paper on a paper route that he's able to improve.

6.   C. Camp out!

The boys unanimously agree that Scotty's question warrants a camp out. They gather together in a huge treehouse for a sleepover and the boys tell the new boy "the legend of the beast."

7.   A. Wendy Peffercorn

Squints has a big crush on Wendy Peffercorn, so he pretends to nearly drown so she'll give him mouth to mouth. After the stunt, the boys are banned for life from the pool. But at the end of the film, the narrator tells us that Squints and Wendy ended up marrying and having nine kids.

QUESTIONS

8. When is the one night of the year when the boys play a night game?

    A. Benny's birthday
    B. July 4th
    C. The first day of summer
    D. The last day of summer

9. What does Bertram bring to the carnival to share with everyone?

    A. Gum
    B. Taffy candy
    C. Chewing tobacco
    D. Bottles of beer

10. What is the "omen" that leads to "the biggest pickle" the boys have ever been in?

    A. Scotty hits a home run
    B. The boys see a shooting star
    C. Squints finds a dollar bill
    D. Benny hits the cover off a ball

11. What is so special about Scotty's stepdad's baseball?

    A. It's signed by Babe Ruth
    B. It's an antique
    C. It was used in the 1961 World Series
    D. It was his first baseball

ANSWERS

8.   B. July 4th

The boys play one night game a year. The fireworks in the sky provide enough light on the sandlot for them to play.

9.   C. Chewing tobacco

Bertram brings a package of chewing tobacco, which all the boys try. They then immediately get on a ride and end up sick. In reality, the "tobacco" was made out of licorice and bacon, and the actors said that chewing it made them almost as sick as their fictional characters were!

10.   D. Benny hits the cover off a ball

When Benny hits the cover off their only baseball, the boys resign themselves to ending their game. But Scotty, wanting to save the day, brings them the baseball his stepfather keeps in his study.

11.   A. It's signed by Babe Ruth

After he brings the ball to the sandlot, Scotty hits his first homerun over the fence into "the beast's" yard. The other boys, who think he should be elated, don't understand his despair over losing the ball until he tells them it was signed by Babe Ruth. Members of the 2015 New York Yankees, including Brett Gardner, Jacoby Ellsbury, and C.C. Sabathia, recreated this scene in tribute to the movie.

QUESTIONS

12. What DON'T the boys try in an effort to get the ball back?

    A. Using vacuum cleaners
    B. Lowering a boy with ropes
    C. Hiding sleeping pills in a steak to knock out "the beast"
    D. Using an erector set

13. Babe Ruth appears to Benny in a dream and tells him to do what about the ball?

    A. "Forget about it"
    B. "Just hop over there and get it"
    C. "Buy a new ball and forge my signature"
    D. "Wait for the ball to come back to you"

14. Whose baseball card does Babe Ruth take from Benny's room in his dream?

    A. Henry Aaron
    B. Lou Gehrig
    C. Mickey Mantle
    D. His own

15. What is the "secret weapon" that Benny uses to retrieve the ball?

    A. A broomstick
    B. A baseball bat
    C. A pair of shoes
    D. A lucky hat

ANSWERS

12.   C. Hiding sleeping pills in a steak to knock out "the beast"

Earlier in the film, Scotty wonders why the kids don't just knock on the door of the home of the junkyard owner when they lose baseballs over his fence, and the boys are terrified that he would suggest such a thing. Later, when they finally meet Mr. Mertle and tell him the story of the Babe Ruth ball, he asks, "Why didn't you just knock on the door?"

13.   B. "Just hop over there and get it"

Babe Ruth in Benny's dream seems to think the solution to the problem is much more simple than the boys have been trying to make it. He tells Benny to "just hop over there and get it," which Benny ends up taking quite literally.

14.   A. Henry Aaron

Ruth sees the baseball card and says, "I don't know why, but can I have this?" Henry Aaron, better known as Hank Aaron, eventually broke Ruth's all-time home run record.

15.   C. A pair of shoes

Benny puts on a new pair of PF Flyers, which, the narrator tells us, are "shoes guaranteed to make a kid run faster and jump higher."

QUESTIONS

16. What happens after Benny grabs the ball and jumps back over the fence?

    A. The boys give him high-fives
    B. The dog breaks free and chases him over the fence
    C. The junkyard owner yells at him
    D. He breaks his ankle

17. Who has a memorable cameo as Mr. Mertle, the junkyard owner?

    A. Kevin Costner
    B. Dennis Quaid
    C. James Earl Jones
    D. Tom Hanks

18. What is the dog's name?

    A. Goliath
    B. Zeus
    C. Colossus
    D. Hercules

19. True or false:

The narrator of the story was the film's director.

20. True or false:

Tom Guiry and Mike Vitar, who played Scotty and Benny, had never met until the day they began filming.

ANSWERS

16.   B. The dog breaks free and chases him over the fence

After chasing Benny all over town, "the beast" ends up trapped under a fence. Scotty and Benny free him, and to everyone's surprise, the huge dog happily licks Scotty's face. To get the shot, the filmmakers covered actor Tom Guiry's face with baby food so the dog would lick it.

17.   C. James Earl Jones

James Earl Jones played the blind owner of the junkyard, who takes pity on Scotty and gives him a ball signed by the entire 1927 Yankee team. The young actors loved working with Jones, and were amazed that "Darth Vader" was actually on set with them!

18.   D. Hercules

Benny tells Scotty that Babe Ruth was the "Hercules of baseball," so it's only fitting that Hercules becomes a mascot for the boys by the end of the film.

19. True

David M. Evans not only directed and narrated the film, but he also co-wrote the script.

20. False

The director wanted the bond between the two boys to seem genuine, so he had them show up to the set weeks early to start rehearsing and getting to know each other. It worked so well that when the rest of the kids arrived to the set to begin shooting, they believed that the two had actually been friends for years.

CENTER STAGE

1. The 2000 film *Center Stage* tells the story of a group of young dancers at a ballet academy. Which actress plays ingénue Jody Sawyer?

    A. Julia Stiles
    B. Amanda Schull
    C. Emilie de Ravin
    D. Neve Campbell

2. Who plays Jody's rebellious friend Eva?

    A. Shannyn Sossamon
    B. Michelle Rodriguez
    C. Jordana Brewster
    D. Zoe Saldana

3. Which actor plays the role of the academy director, Jonathan Reeves?

    A. Kelsey Grammer
    B. Patrick Stewart
    C. Peter Gallagher
    D. Saul Rubinek

ANSWERS

1.   B. Amanda Schull

Schull was dancing with the San Francisco Ballet when she was cast for Center Stage, *which was her screen debut. Since then, she has gone on to appear in* One Tree Hill, Pretty Little Liars, *and* Suits, *and she stars in the Syfy channel show* 12 Monkeys.

2.   D. Zoe Saldana

Saldana developed a love for dance while living in the Dominican Republic as an adolescent. Her big break in Center Stage *led to even bigger opportunities in block-busters like* Avatar, Star Trek, *and* Guardians of the Galaxy.

3.   C. Peter Gallagher

Prior to Center Stage, *Gallagher had a memorable role as the comatose man Sandra Bullock falls for in* While You Were Sleeping. *He has since gone on to star in* The O.C. *and* Covert Affairs, *and reprised his role as Reeves for* Center Stage: Turn It Up, *and* Center Stage: Dance Camp.

QUESTIONS

4. What is the name of the company the dancers are hoping to join?

    A. American Ballet Company
    B. New York Ballet Company
    C. American Dance Theater
    D. Ballet of New York

5. The interior shots for the movie were shot on location at which school?

    A. The Juilliard School
    B. Columbia University
    C. Joffrey Ballet School
    D. The School of American Ballet

6. Which Olympic figure skater appears in the film as Russian dancer Sergei?

    A. Alexei Yagudin
    B. Ilia Kulik
    C. Alexei Urmanov
    D. Viktor Petrenko

7. After she arrives at the school, Jody meets a group of new friends, including Eva, Russian dancer Sergei, friendly Erik, and uptight Maureen. She also falls for the "bad boy" persona of which dancer?

    A. Connor Nelson
    B. Kevin Nicholson
    C. Kelvin Niles
    D. Cooper Nielson

ANSWERS

4.   A. American Ballet Company

The American Ballet Company doesn't actually exist, but the mood of the film is said to resemble both the American Ballet Theater and the New York City Ballet.

5.   C. Joffrey Ballet School

While the interiors were shot at Joffrey Ballet School, the exterior of the American Ballet Academy at the beginning of the film was shot at the Juilliard School.

6.   B. Ilia Kulik

Kulik won a gold medal in Men's Figure Skating in the 1998 Winter Olympics in Nagano, Japan. He has been called "the Leonardo DiCaprio of Figure Skating" because of his charm and good looks.

7.   D. Cooper Nielson

In one scene, Cooper, played by dancer Ethan Stiefel, rudely brushes off the smitten Jody by leaving a performance with another girl. The girl was played by Stiefel's then-fiancée, ballerina Gillian Murphy.

QUESTIONS

8. What does Erik say is his stage name?

    A. Erik O. Jones
    B. Erik J. Jones
    C. Erik E. Evans
    D. Erik Erikson

9. What is the name of the former prima ballerina who is now the girls' instructor?

    A. Emily
    B. Kathleen
    C. Juliette
    D. Anna

10. Who is the "good guy" who takes an interest in Jody?

    A. Thomas
    B. Charlie
    C. Billy
    D. Michael

11. What does the group do for Erik's birthday?

    A. Go on a boat ride
    B. Visit a salsa club
    C. Visit the Empire State Building
    D. Go out to dinner

ANSWERS

8.   A. Erik O. Jones

Erik, played by Shakiem Evans, tells the group that "the O stands for Oprah."

9.   C. Juliette

Although the instructor goes by Juliette Simone, Maureen's overbearing mother condescendingly remarks that, "her real name's Julie Simon, she's from Perth Amboy, and her father managed a Walmart."

10.   B. Charlie

Unlike Cooper, Charlie genuinely cares about Jody and her feelings. Fortunately, she wises up at the end of the film and tells Cooper that "you're an amazing dancer and a great choreographer, but as a boyfriend, you kinda suck," before running off to celebrate with Charlie.

11.   A. Go on a boat ride

The group takes a Circle Line sightseeing tour, which is a cruise that sails around the island of Manhattan.

QUESTIONS

12. What is the name of Maureen's med-student love interest?

    A. Johnny
    B. Jordan
    C. Jack
    D. Jim

13. What song do the dancers warm up to during the jazz class Jody takes?

    A. "Oops!. . . I Did It Again" by Britney Spears
    B. "Bye Bye Bye" by 'N Sync
    C. "Candy" by Mandy Moore
    D. "Every Morning" by Sugar Ray

14. Who was originally going to star alongside Jody in Cooper's workshop ballet?

    A. Erik and Cooper
    B. Erik and Charlie
    C. Sergei and Charlie
    D. Sergei and Erik

15. What color is Jody's outfit in the final scene of her workshop performance?

    A. Blue
    B. Green
    C. Red
    D. White

ANSWERS

12.   D. Jim

Jim, a Columbia pre-med student, is played by Eion Bailey. Bailey has appeared on ER, Covert Affairs, *and* Once Upon a Time, *and in the HBO miniseries* Band of Brothers.

13.   C. Candy, by Mandy Moore

Moore also contributed to the soundtrack of Center Stage with the ballad "I Wanna Be With You."

14.   B. Erik and Charlie

Cooper's ballet begins as a dance starring Jody, Erik, and Charlie, but Erik twists his ankle during the rehearsal. Cooper decides to dance Erik's part, leading to a pas de troix *between Jody, Charlie, and Cooper. This mirrors the love triangle drama in their real (fictional) lives.*

15.   C. Red

Jody's final outfit is red, including her shoes. But when the scene opens, the camera is zoomed in on her shoes, which are light, pearly pink. When we next see a shot of her, the shoes are red. Oops!

QUESTIONS

16. True or false:

At the end of the film, we discover that Jody was accepted into the American Ballet Company.

17. True or false:

Susan May Pratt was cast to play the best dancer in the school, Maureen, even though she had no training as a dancer.

18. Finish the quote:

"You didn't have the feet. I don't have the _____."

ANSWERS

16. False

We actually never find out whether or not she was accepted. She opts to not even hear the decision that Jonathan and Juliette have made, and instead accepts a position as a principal dancer with Cooper's company.

17. True

Unlike the other dancers in the film, Pratt had no dance training before she was cast. This explains why the "best dancer in the school" is barely seen dancing in the movie!

18. Heart

Maureen's controlling mother, who left a dancing career because of her bad feet, pressures her daughter into pursuing ballet. When Maureen finally realizes she doesn't have the heart to keep going, she offers her role in Jonathan's workshop ballet to Eva, who surprises everyone with an outstanding performance. Maureen finally confronts her mother and tells her she is giving up ballet.

CONGO

1. Who directed the 1995 action adventure film *Congo?*

    A. Frank Marshall
    B. Robert Zemeckis
    C. Ron Howard
    D. Michael Mann

2. Who wrote the novel on which the movie is based?

    A. Isaac Asimov
    B. Douglas Preston
    C. Michael Crichton
    D. Robin Cook

3. In the beginning of the film, we meet Charles Travis, an employee for the TraviCom communications company. Which cult-favorite actor plays this small role?

    A. Lance Henriksen
    B. Tom Noonan
    C. Robert Englund
    D. Bruce Campbell

ANSWERS

1.   A. Frank Marshall

In addition to directing several films, Marshall is well known for producing quite a few blockbusters. His credits include Raiders of the Lost Ark, Poltergeist, Back to the Future, The Bourne Identity, *and* Jurassic World.

2.   C. Michael Crichton

Many of Crichton's novels have been developed into films, including Sphere, Jurassic Park, *and* Timeline.

3.   D. Bruce Campbell

Campbell has said that he did not enjoy working with screenwriter John Patrick Shanley, because Shanley refused to allow ad-libbing on the set!

QUESTIONS

4. Which actress plays Charles' ex-fiancée and former CIA operative, Dr. Karen Ross?

    A. Laura Linney
    B. Mary-Louise Parker
    C. Bridget Fonda
    D. Penelope Ann Miller

5. What were Charles and his team looking for in the Congo?

    A. Iron
    B. Diamonds
    C. Copper
    D. Oil

6. Which actor plays Herkermer Homolka, a supposedly wealthy Romanian philanthropist, who turns out to be a treasure seeker?

    A. Tim Curry
    B. Anthony Hopkins
    C. Danny DeVito
    D. Willem Dafoe

7. Dylan Walsh, known for his role as Dr. Sean McNamara on *Nip/Tuck*, plays which character in *Congo*?

    A. Bob Driscoll
    B. Eddie Ventro
    C. Peter Elliot
    D. Boyd Travis

ANSWERS

4.   A. Laura Linney

After her performance in the critically panned Congo, *Linney would go on to receive three Oscar nominations – for her work in the films* You Can Count on Me, Kinsey, *and* The Savages.

5.   B. Diamonds

Charles and his team are sent to the Congo by his father, R.B. Travis, who wants them to find a rare blue diamond which will enhance their communications abilities.

6.   A. Tim Curry

Not only was the movie itself almost universally reviled, but Curry's "Romanian" accent was ridiculed, as well. The website Geekscape *placed him on their list of "The Top Five Worst Movie Accents," along with Sean Connery in* The Hunt for Red October *and Kevin Costner in* Robin Hood: Prince of Thieves. *Now that's a bad accent!*

7.   C. Peter Elliot

Walsh plays Dr. Peter Elliot, a primatologist who works with a gorilla named Amy. Interestingly, Peter Elliot is a real person who works as a gorilla choreographer and ape performer. He has been in many films, including Gorillas in the Mist, The Island of Dr. Moreau, *and, of course,* Congo.

QUESTIONS

8. What species of gorilla is Amy?

    A. Silverback
    B. Mountain
    C. Lowland
    D. Western

9. What is Amy's favorite color?

    A. Red
    B. Blue
    C. Yellow
    D. Green

10. What drink is served to Amy on the plane ride to Africa?

    A. Warm milk
    B. Martini
    C. Banana smoothie
    D. Tea

11. Who plays Captain Munro Kelly, the mercenary who leads the group through the jungle?

    A. Ernie Hudson
    B. Delroy Lindo
    C. Mykelti Williamson
    D. Ving Rhames

ANSWERS

8.   B. Mountain

In the film, Amy is a mountain gorilla. But in reality, there are no mountain gorillas in captivity, and the few that have been taken to zoos have died quickly.

9.   D. Green

When we first see Amy, she is painting pictures with research assistant Richard (Grant Heslov). He mentions that green is her favorite color, and most of her paintings reflect the green of the jungle.

10.   B. Martini

Amy uses her sign language to demand a "green drop drink," which turns out to be a martini with green olives. Dr. Elliot says she's allowed to have one because it will calm her down for the flight.

11.   A. Ernie Hudson

Hudson, perhaps best known for his role as Winston Zeddemore in Ghostbusters, *has said that Munro Kelly is one of his favorite characters that he's played throughout his career.*

QUESTIONS

12. How does the team get into Zaire when their plane is attacked?

A. They manage to land safely in Zaire
B. They turn around and then hike over the border through the jungle
C. They use parachutes
D. They drive

13. What is the name of the lost city that Homolka is searching for?

A. Zinj
B. Zinn
C. Djinn
D. Zulu

14. What is the symbol for the lost city?

A. A diamond
B. An open eye
C. A palm branch
D. A pyramid

15. How much does Karen say the equipment from Charles' camp weighed?

A. 200 pounds
B. 250 pounds
C. 300 pounds
D. 400 pounds

ANSWERS

12.   C. They use parachutes

Zaire is now known as the Democratic Republic of the Congo, and it has a long history of political instability. In the film, the group's plane is attacked with rockets and they must use parachutes to escape. In typical movie fashion, the plane is destroyed as soon as they are safely on the ground.

13.   A. Zinj

Homolka is searching for legendary King Solomon's diamonds in the lost city of Zinj.

14.   B. An open eye

The open eye symbol is seen throughout the film. Amy draws it in her paintings of the jungle, Homolka has a ring with the symbol on it, and when the group finds the lost temple, it is carved into the rock of the structure.

15.   C. 300 pounds

The group only stumbles upon Charles' abandoned camp because they set off a perimeter alarm. Everything from the camp is gone, and Karen wonders aloud how 300 pounds of equipment could disappear.

QUESTIONS

16. What do the hieroglyphics in the temple mean?

      A. We are watching you
      B. We see you
      C. Leave this place
      D. Woe to all who enter here

17. What is blocking the exit from the diamond mine?

      A. A giant boulder
      B. A geode
      C. A river of lava
      D. Stalactites

18. What does Karen do at the end of the film when she finds out Charles' father only wanted the diamond and didn't care about finding his son?

      A. Quits her job
      B. Throws the diamond at the monitor screen
      C. Destroys the communications satellite with the laser
      D. Reports TraviCom to the FCC

19. True or false:

"Margaritaville" singer Jimmy Buffett is in this film.

ANSWERS

16.   A. We are watching you

Homolka translates the hieroglyphics after the "mythical killer apes" attack the camp. The group comes to the conclusion that humans taught the gorillas how to protect the temple and its diamond mine, and the humans were the ones "watching" the apes. Eventually, the gorillas turned on their human masters, but continued to protect the mine.

17.   B. A geode

When Karen sees the geode blocking their exit she calls it "a giant diamond." But in actuality, quartz and calcite are the most commonly found minerals in geodes.

18.   C. Destroys the communications satellite with the laser

At the beginning of the film, Karen tells R.B. that if he's lying about only wanting to find his son, she'll make him sorry. Upon finding out his son is dead, he shows no remorse – he is only concerned about the diamond. So Karen makes good on her promise and destroys his satellite.

19. True

Buffett has a cameo as the 727 pilot. The singer has had small appearances in several other films, including Repo Man, Hook, *and* Cobb. *And in the 2015 film* Jurassic World, *Buffett is seen as a tourist holding two margaritas when the dinosaurs attack. Buffett is a licensed pilot in real life!*

HUDSON HAWK

1. Which actor plays the title character in 1991's action comedy *Hudson Hawk?*

    A. Tom Hanks
    B. Mel Gibson
    C. Bill Paxton
    D. Bruce Willis

2. The film was directed by *Heathers* director Michael Lehmann, and produced by which action-movie producer?

    A. Jerry Bruckheimer
    B. Joel Silver
    C. Don Simpson
    D. Brian Grazer

3. What is Hudson Hawk's real name?

    A. Freddie Hawk
    B. Eddie Hawkins
    C. Larry Harris
    D. Teddy Hudson

ANSWERS

1.   D. Bruce Willis

Hudson Hawk *also marks Willis' first and, as of 2016, only film writing credit. He co-wrote the story with Robert Kraft, who was the film's composer.*

2.   B. Joel Silver

Silver is well-known for producing films such as Lethal Weapon, Predator, *and* Die Hard. *Willis was eager for him to helm the project because of his "hands on" approach to filmmaking.*

3.   B. Eddie Hawkins

The nickname "Hudson Hawk" comes from the name for the brisk winds that blow off the Hudson river in New York City.

QUESTIONS

4. Hudson was in prison for ten years, which was so long that he's never heard of what?

    A. The Simpsons
    B. New Kids on the Block
    C. Nintendo
    D. Bon Jovi

5. Who plays Hudson's sidekick, Tommy Five-Tone?

    A. Danny Aiello
    B. Joe Pesci
    C. Paul Sorvino
    D. Dennis Farina

6. What does Hudson most want to drink after being released from prison?

    A. Beer
    B. Cappuccino
    C. Scotch
    D. Orange juice

7. In the film, New Jersey's third largest crime family is known as what?

    A. The Sopranos
    B. The Italians
    C. The Mario Brothers
    D. The Godfathers

ANSWERS

4.   C. Nintendo

There was actually a game released for Nintendo to coincide with the movie. Players would take on the role of Hudson Hawk and attempt to steal artifacts without setting off alarms.

5.   A. Danny Aiello

Aiello was the filmmakers' first choice for the role, since he and Willis had known each other for years and wanted to work together. Aiello was excited to work on the project, and even postponed his work on another film so he could join the cast of Hudson Hawk.

6.   B. Cappuccino

When Tommy picks up Hudson at the prison, he meets him with a cappuccino, but it immediately spills before Hudson has a chance to drink it. His attempts to enjoy a cup of his favorite beverage are continually foiled, until he is finally able to drink his coffee in the final scene.

7.   C. The Mario Brothers

This is the second Nintendo reference in the film, as Super Mario Bros. *was a game available for the console. Incidentally, Cesar Mario, one of the Mario Brothers, was played by Frank Stallone, the brother of Sylvester Stallone.*

QUESTIONS

8. Who plays eccentric billionaire villainess Minerva Mayflower?

    A. Tilda Swinton
    B. Madonna
    C. Jamie Lee Curtis
    D. Sandra Bernhard

9. What is the name of the model of the horse that the Mayflowers want Hudson to steal?

    A. Sfuzzi
    B. Sforza
    C. Sfumato
    D. Spumoni

10. Hudson and Tommy sing songs in order to track their time during heists. What is the song they sing when they break into the auction house?

    A. "Swinging on a Star"
    B. "When You Wish Upon a Star"
    C. "Some Enchanted Evening"
    D. "Mr. Sandman"

11. Hudson is attracted to Anna Baragli, played by Andie MacDowell. He's disappointed when he finds out she's what?

    A. Married
    B. A nun
    C. His sister
    D. Engaged

ANSWERS

8.   D. Sandra Bernhard

When the film was released, a Washington Post review said Bernhard "walks away with the movie on her sensational entrance, supplying its only real comic energy." This was high praise for the film her costar, Richard E. Grant, called "a stinking pile of steaming hot donkey droppings."

9.   B. Sforza

The name comes from the House of Sforza, a ruling family in Renaissance Italy in Milan. In reality, the clay model of the horse was destroyed by French soldiers invading Milan in 1499.

10.   A. Swinging on a Star

Tommy tells Hudson that they have "five minutes and change" to finish their heist, yet in reality, the version of the song they sing would only last about 2 minutes and 30 seconds.

11.   B. A nun

In a confusing turn of events, Anna is also an operative who works for a secret counter-espionage agency at the Vatican. The Vatican and the CIA agree to help Hawk in his mission to steal da Vinci artifacts, but Anna's intent is to foil the plot.

QUESTIONS

12. Which is NOT one of the CIA's "candy bar" henchmen?

    A. Snickers
    B. Almond Joy
    C. Butterfinger
    D. Milky Way

13. The Mayflowers fly Hudson to which city?

    A. Rome
    B. Florence
    C. Venice
    D. Milan

14. After Anna gets drugged, she says she has to speak to whom?

    A. The Pope
    B. The President
    C. The dolphins
    D. The elephants

15. At the end of the movie, how do Hawk and Anna escape the castle before it blows up?

    A. They jump out a window
    B. They use da Vinci's flying machine
    C. They rappel down a wall with ropes
    D. They find a secret passage

ANSWERS

12.   D. Milky Way

*In addition to Snickers, Almond Joy, and Butterfinger, the "candy bars" include Kit Kat, played by a pre-*NYPD Blue *and* CSI: Miami *David Caruso.*

13.   A. Rome

Unluckily for Hawk, his flight is anything but first class. He is surprised with an injection of sleeping serum, then unceremoniously tossed into a crate and flown overseas.

14.   C. The dolphins

In a random drug-induced haze, Anna proclaims that she must speak with the dolphins, and then proceeds to squeal in high-pitched "dolphin language." She also wonders, "What does the color blue taste like?"

15.   B. They use da Vinci's flying machine

Leonardo da Vinci actually did sketch out ideas for flying machines based on the anatomy of birds and bats. They would have been unlikely to fly, but his work inspired aeronauts hundreds of years later.

QUESTIONS

16. True or false:

Although the movie was a critical failure, it did well at the box office.

17. True or false:

The "Leonardo da Vinci Gold Machine," a machine that turns lead into gold through the use of solar energy and alchemical salts, was actually described in da Vinci's own notes.

18. When Hudson Hawk says his coffee "doesn't taste like cappuccino," Anna says, "Oh, I guess I put too much _____ in it."

ANSWERS

16. False

The film had a $65 million budget, but ended up grossing only $17 million at the box office.

17. False

Although Leonardo da Vinci envisioned many things that were far ahead of his time, the machine depicted in the film was dreamed up by production designer Jackson De Govia. He tried to stay true to the imagination of da Vinci, stating, "In producing the gold machine, I was able to incorporate and adapt mechanical principles and devices that came directly from the mind and pen of Leonardo da Vinci."

18. Ethyl Chloride

After taking a sip, Hawk passes out. This could be considered a "movie goof," as it would take much more than a sip of ethyl chloride to render someone unconscious.

INDIANA JONES
THE KINGDOM OF THE CRYSTAL SKULL

1. Harrison Ford, of course, plays the titular role in *Indiana Jones and the Kingdom of the Crystal Skull*. How old was he when the film was released?

> A. 63
> B. 65
> C. 66
> D. 68

2. Which popular director helmed the film?

> A. George Lucas
> B. James Cameron
> C. Steven Spielberg
> D. Peter Jackson

3. Who composed the score for the film, including the famous "Raiders March" theme music?

> A. John Williams
> B. James Horner
> C. Hans Zimmer
> D. John Barry

ANSWERS

1.   B. 65

Ford was 65 when the movie premiered. Regardless, he was reportedly in such good shape that his measurements for his costumes hadn't changed since Indiana Jones and the Last Crusade, *filmed almost 20 years before.*

2.   C. Steven Spielberg

Spielberg also directed the first three Indiana Jones movies. He opted not to film Indiana Jones and the Kingdom of the Crystal Skull *in a digital format, wanting to preserve the same look as the previous films.*

3.   A. John Williams

Williams has composed some of the most recognizable music in the world of film, including themes for Jaws, Star Wars, Superman, *and* Home Alone. *Incidentally, the character of Mutt Williams in* Indiana Jones and the Kingdom of the Crystal Skull *was named in honor of the composer.*

QUESTIONS

4. In the very first scene of the movie, we see a group of teenagers racing their car in and out of a line of army vehicles, attempting to goad them into drag racing. What song is playing during the scene?

      A. "Rock Around the Clock"
      B. "Hound Dog"
      C. "Good Golly Miss Molly"
      D. "Great Balls of Fire"

5. In previous Indiana Jones movies, Nazis were often the villains. Who are the villains in this film?

      A. Colombian drug lords
      B. Ex-Nazis
      C. The Soviets
      D. Washington politicians

6. When Indy first escapes from the Russians, he runs to a small town and knocks on the door of a house. What does he find inside?

      A. A pack of vicious dogs
      B. An eerie family of mannequins
      C. A startled family eating dinner
      D. Nothing, the house is empty

7. Who plays the role of villainess Irina Spalko?

      A. Liv Tyler
      B. Tilda Swinton
      C. Charlize Theron
      D. Cate Blanchett

ANSWERS

4.   B. *Hound Dog*

Hound Dog *was made popular by Elvis Presley in 1956. The song immediately sets the scene for the 50s timeframe of the movie action.*

5.   C. The Soviets

Ford stated that they'd "plumb wore the Nazis out" by the time the fourth film was made. Spielberg agreed, opting to make Cold-War-era Soviets the villains in the story. He hired Russian actors to play the parts of the Russian soldiers, so their accents would be authentic.

6.   B. An eerie family of mannequins

Indy has managed to stumble upon an atomic bomb test site. In one of the most-ridiculed scenes of the film, he wedges himself into a lead-lined refrigerator and survives the blast, which most scientists agree would be impossible. But maybe it doesn't matter for the sake of the story. After all, when have Indiana Jones movies been about scientific accuracy?

7.   D. Cate Blanchett

Blanchett took fencing and karate lessons to prepare for her performance. She based Irina Spalko's mannerisms on Rosa Klebb from the James Bond film From Russia With Love.

QUESTIONS

8. Which actor plays the part of motorcycle-riding greaser Mutt Williams?

    A. Shia LaBeouf
    B. Robert Pattinson
    C. Aaron Taylor-Johnson
    D. Andrew Garfield

9. Which previous Indiana Jones movie character makes an appearance in this film?

    A. Sallah
    B. Willie Scott
    C. Marion Ravenwood
    D. Short Round

10. What is the name of the diner where Indy and Mutt talk about the disappearance of Harold Oxley?

    A. Ted's
    B. Arnie's
    C. Joe's
    D. Brando's

11. Which *Alien* actor appears as Professor Oxley?

    A. Ian Holm
    B. Harry Dean Stanton
    C. John Hurt
    D. Tom Skerritt

ANSWERS

8.   A. Shia LaBeouf

LaBeouf was so excited about the prospect of appearing in an Indiana Jones film that he didn't even read the script before he agreed to play the part!

9.   C. Marion Ravenwood

Marion, played by Karen Allen, returns as Indy's love interest. Spielberg considered also bringing back John Rhys-Davies as Sallah for a brief cameo, but Rhys-Davies declined.

10.   B. Arnie's

The diner in the film was named after Spielberg's father, Arnold Spielberg.

11.   C. John Hurt

In the 1979 science fiction thriller Alien, *Hurt played the part of Kane, the first to succumb to the wrath of the alien in the infamous "chestburster" scene. Unlike LaBeouf, Hurt insisted on reading the script for* Indiana Jones and the Kingdom of the Crystal Skull *before agreeing to play the part of Oxley.*

QUESTIONS

12. When Indy and Mutt are in Peru and find the cell in which Oxley had been kept, what word had been scrawled on the walls in many languages?

    A. Help
    B. Rescue
    C. Heal
    D. Return

13. When does Indy find out that Mutt is his son?

    A. When they first speak in the diner
    B. When he and Marion are stuck in a sand pit
    C. In the back of a truck when they're being chased by Irina
    D. After he and Marion get married

14. When the group reaches Akator, how do they get past the natives who are guarding the temple?

    A. They show them the crystal skull
    B. Mutt points a gun at them
    C. Oxley reasons with them in their own language
    D. Indy disarms them with his whip

15. After returning the skull to the temple, the aliens, speaking through Oxley's interpretation of their language, say they want to give the humans a gift. What does Irina demand?

    A. Power
    B. Wealth
    C. Knowledge
    D. Long life

ANSWERS

12.   D. Return

Oxley had written the word "return" over and over in his cell at the sanatorium. Eventually Indy discovers that Oxley was being influenced by the crystal skull, which wanted to be returned to the Temple of Akator.

13.   B. When he and Marion are stuck in a sand pit

At a very inopportune time – when she and Indy are sinking in a pit of sand – Marion reveals that Mutt's real name is Henry Walton Jones III.

14.   A. They show them the crystal skull

When the natives appear, ready to block anyone who attempts to pass, Indy asks Oxley what they can do. Oxley unwraps the crystal skull, and the natives back away from it, allowing the group to pass.

15.   C. Knowledge

Irina demands to "know everything," but the knowledge she is given overwhelms her, and she disintegrates. This continues the pattern in Indiana Jones films of the villain succumbing to their own greed and being destroyed through supernatural means.

QUESTIONS

16. What happens with Indy's job at the university at the end of the film?

        A. He retires
        B. He is fired
        C. He returns to find everything exactly the same
        D. He is promoted to associate dean

17. True or false:

This was the first Indiana Jones film not to receive any Academy Award nominations.

18. True or false:

Steven Spielberg's daughter, Sasha, appears in the film.

19. True or false:

As with all of the previous Indiana Jones films, Indy makes a stop in Asia during his travels.

ANSWERS

16.   D. He is promoted to associate dean

Indy's long-awaited marriage to Marion isn't the only happy occurrence at the end of the film. We also see a worker applying Indy's new title to the window of his office door.

17. True

The previous films were nominated for at least two Oscars each. Indiana Jones and the Temple of Doom *and* Indiana Jones and the Last Crusade *each won one Oscar, and* Raiders of the Lost Ark *won four.*

18. True

Sasha Spielberg plays the part of the girl who punches Mutt in the diner scene. She is the daughter of Spielberg and Kate Capshaw, who played Willie Scott in Indiana Jones and the Temple of Doom.

19. False

This is actually the first film where Indy does not visit Asia. In Raiders of the Lost Ark, *he visits Nepal; in* Indiana Jones and the Temple of Doom, *he visits China and India; and in* Indiana Jones and the Last Crusade, *Indy discovers the Holy Grail in Hatay.*

LAYER CAKE

1. Which actor stars in the 2004 crime drama *Layer Cake?*

    A. Hugh Jackman
    B. Daniel Craig
    C. Sam Rockwell
    D. Gerard Butler

2. The name of Craig's character is never mentioned in the film, and he is referred to only as XXXX. What illegal enterprise does XXXX deal with?

    A. Weapons
    B. Stolen cars
    C. Drugs
    D. Money laundering

3. What is the name of XXXX's friend and henchman who watches his back?

    A. Marty
    B. Mark
    C. Morton
    D. Morty

ANSWERS

1.   B. Daniel Craig

Producer Barbara Broccoli saw Craig in Layer Cake *and thought he might be a good fit as the new James Bond. He debuted in the role of Bond in 2006's* Casino Royale.

2.   C. Drugs

At the beginning of the film, XXXX is hard at work preparing a stash of cocaine, but he doesn't consider himself "a gangster." Rather, he calls himself "a businessman whose commodity happens to be cocaine."

3.   D. Morty

Morty is played by George Harris, who has appeared in films like Raiders of the Lost Ark, Black Hawk Down, *and* The Interpreter, *but perhaps is best known for his role in the* Harry Potter *films as Kingsley Shacklebolt.*

QUESTIONS

4. What are XXXX's plans for the immediate future at the beginning of the film?

    A. Retirement
    B. Doubling his operation
    C. Buying a bigger house
    D. Hiding from his boss

5. What is the name of the character who XXXX describes as Jimmy Price's "right hand man"?

    A. Joe
    B. Gene
    C. Johnny
    D. Gerard

6. Which *Batman* movie actor has a small role as Clarkie?

    A. Gary Oldman
    B. Joseph Gordon-Levitt
    C. Christian Bale
    D. Tom Hardy

7. Who is the leader of the "loud wannabe gangsters" who steal a shipment of Ecstasy pills?

    A. Slasher
    B. The Duke
    C. Terry
    D. Tiptoes

ANSWERS

4.   A. Retirement

XXXX is hoping to retire from the drug business, but before he can bow out, he and Morty are asked to one final lunch by their head supplier, Jimmy Price (Kenneth Cranham).

5.   B. Gene

Gene is played by Irish actor Colm Meaney, known to Star Trek *fans for his role as oft-suffering Chief Miles O'Brien on* Star Trek: The Next Generation *and* Star Trek: Deep Space Nine.

6.   D. Tom Hardy

Hardy appeared as the villain Bane in 2012's The Dark Knight Rises. *He is also known for his work in films like* Inception, Mad Max: Fury Road, *and* The Revenant.

7.   B. The Duke

The Duke unwisely hijacks a shipment of one million Ecstasy pills from a gang of Serbian war criminals. Jimmy Price then asks XXXX to purchase and distribute the pills himself.

QUESTIONS

8. In addition to the Ecstasy drug deal, what other favor does Jimmy Price ask of XXXX over lunch?

    A. Locate a missing girl
    B. Help him buy a house
    C. Sell more cocaine
    D. Hide some weapons

9. What is the name of the Duke's nephew?

    A. Terry
    B. Gazza
    C. Sidney
    D. Brian

10. What is the name of XXXX's love interest in the film?

    A. Tammy
    B. Tina
    C. Teresa
    D. Terri

11. When XXXX and his men find Charlie's boyfriend, Kinky, what is wrong with him?

    A. He is delirious
    B. His leg is broken
    C. He is dead from an overdose
    D. He has amnesia

ANSWERS

8.   A. Locate a missing girl

Price asks XXXX to find Charlie, the daughter of his friend Eddie Temple. According to Price, a drug-addicted Charlie fled a rehabilitation center with her boyfriend, Kinky.

9.   C. Sidney

Sidney is played by actor Ben Whishaw, who plays Q in the James Bond movies alongside Craig. They also worked together in the films The Trench *and* Enduring Love.

10.   A. Tammy

XXXX runs into Sidney at a bar, where he is with his girlfriend, Tammy, played by Sienna Miller. XXXX is immediately smitten, and Tammy slips him her number when Sidney isn't looking.

11.   C. He is dead from an overdose

After interrogating Kinky's crackhead roommates, the men learn that Charlie has supposedly gone to Brighton. And although it appears that Kinky has overdosed, his roommates are convinced that he was murdered.

QUESTIONS

12. What is the name of the hitman hired by the Serbians?

    A. Draco
    B. Dragan
    C. Drake
    D. Dimitri

13. What does XXXX borrow from Gene?

    A. A pistol
    B. A knife
    C. A rifle
    D. An axe

14. Who has XXXX kidnapped as he is getting ready for his tryst with Tammy?

    A. Jimmy Price
    B. The Duke
    C. Eddie Temple
    D. Sidney

15. What does XXXX do when he finds out that Jimmy Price set him up?

    A. Destroys the Ecstasy pills
    B. Steals his car
    C. Leaves the country with Tammy
    D. Shoots him

ANSWERS

12.   B. Dragan

The hitman was played by an actor who is actually named Dragan Micanovic. He is a Serbian actor who has appeared in English-language films like Bad Company *and* RocknRolla, *in addition to* Layer Cake.

13.   A. A pistol

In the DVD commentary, director Matthew Vaughn says that in this scene, XXXX "wants to be James Bond." A year after Layer Cake *was released, Craig was announced as Pierce Brosnan's successor in the James Bond franchise.*

14.   C. Eddie Temple

The part of Temple is played by prolific actor Michael Gambon, who has been working in television and film since the 1960s. Gambon gained worldwide fame for his role as Professor Albus Dumbledore in the Harry Potter *films.*

15.   D. Shoots him

XXXX kills Jimmy with the pistol he borrowed from Gene, not realizing that Gene previously used it to murder someone. Gene attacks XXXX when he finds out, until XXXX is able to convince him that Jimmy was a snitch.

QUESTIONS

16. What happens to the sniper XXXX hires to kill the hitman, Dragan?

    A. Dragan kills him
    B. He runs away
    C. He kills the wrong man
    D. He never shows up

17. How does XXXX manage to appease Dragan?

    A. Pays him a large sum of money
    B. Offers to share the Ecstasy profit with him
    C. Gives him the Duke's head
    D. He shoots him with Gene's pistol

18. What happens to XXXX at the end of the film?

    A. He finally retires
    B. He is shot by Sidney
    C. He decides to keep working
    D. He flees the country

19. True or false:

Although the gang of criminals in the greenhouse are said to be Serbian, the leader, Slavo, speaks Romanian to his men.

ANSWERS

16.   A. Dragan kills him

In a twist, the target of the sniper becomes a sniper himself. In the book on which the movie is based, by author J.J. Connolly, the sniper accidentally kills an American tourist. The scene was changed for the film, which the director has stated works even better for the story.

17.   C. Gives him the Duke's head

At the end of the film, XXXX stages a fake police raid on the warehouse where the Ecstasy pills are being held, knowing that Dragan will see it and believe the pills are in the hands of the police. He also presents the hitman with the Duke's head, which Dragan takes to his Serbian bosses as proof that the man who stole from them is dead.

18.   B. He is shot by Sidney

XXXX meets Tammy outside of a country club, ready to begin his retirement and his new life. But a jealous Sidney shows up and shoots him in the chest. The original ending had XXXX and Tammy driving off together into the sunset, but the director decided it was too cliché. But interestingly, we don't actually see XXXX die, so his fate is unknown.

19. True

Marcel Iures, the actor who plays Slavo, is a Romanian actor who spoke in his native language. Apparently the filmmakers knew that most people viewing the film wouldn't know the difference between Serbian and Romanian!

THE PROFESSIONAL

1. Who directed the 1994 crime drama *The Professional?*

    A. Ridley Scott
    B. David Lynch
    C. Gore Verbinski
    D. Luc Besson

2. Who plays the part of the professional assassin, Leon?

    A. Jean Reno
    B. Robert De Niro
    C. Liam Neeson
    D. Jason Statham

3. Which popular actress makes her feature film debut as Leon's young neighbor, Mathilda?

    A. Mila Kunis
    B. Scarlett Johansson
    C. Anne Hathaway
    D. Natalie Portman

ANSWERS

1. **D. Luc Besson**

Besson also co-produced the film and wrote the script, and has written screenplays for dozens of films, including The Fifth Element, The Transporter, Taken, *and* Lucy.

2. **A. Jean Reno**

Reno and Besson have worked together on many projects, including the films Subway, The Big Blue, *and* La Femme Nikita.

3. **D. Natalie Portman**

Portman was originally considered too young for the role, but eventually won out over 2000 other girls. She was 11 years old when she was cast.

QUESTIONS

4. Which actor plays corrupt DEA agent Stansfield?

    A. Viggo Mortensen
    B. Gary Oldman
    C. Michael Madsen
    D. Ralph Fiennes

5. Where does the story take place?

    A. Paris
    B. Los Angeles
    C. New York City
    D. Rome

6. After Stansfield interrogates Mathilda's father about the drugs, when does he tell him he'll be back?

    A. At midnight
    B. The next day at noon
    C. In 48 hours
    D. On Monday

7. Who is Stansfield's favorite composer?

    A. Beethoven
    B. Mozart
    C. Bach
    D. Schubert

ANSWERS

4. **B. Gary Oldman**

Oldman's portrayal of Stansfield was called "the role that launched a thousand villains" by MSN Movies. He would later appear as another eccentric villain, Jean-Baptiste Emanuel Zorg, in Besson's film The Fifth Element.

5. **C. New York City**

Although the movie takes place in New York City, the interiors of Leon's apartment were actually filmed in Paris.

6. **B. The next day at noon**

One of Besson's trademarks is to film a scene in real time. Right before Stansfield and his men return, we see a clock in Leon's apartment that reads 11:58. The scene that follows takes exactly two minutes, after which Stansfield and his men return.

7. **A. Beethoven**

The scene where Stansfield talks about his love of the composer's music was completely improvised by Oldman!

QUESTIONS

8. Who is the only family member Mathilda really cares about?

    A. Her mother
    B. Her father
    C. Her sister
    D. Her brother

9. What word does Leon use to describe his profession?

    A. Scrubber
    B. Fixer
    C. Cleaner
    D. Duster

10. What is Leon's drink of choice?

    A. Milk
    B. Orange juice
    C. Wine
    D. Scotch

11. What is Leon's most important rule for his profession?

    A. Leave no fingerprints
    B. No women, no kids
    C. Always wear a mask
    D. Don't fall in love

ANSWERS

8.   D. Her brother

Mathilda's abusive father helps Stansfield with his drug trade, and she is not fond of her half-sister and stepmother. Her younger brother is the only family member she feels connected to, so when Stansfield kills him, she wants revenge.

9.   C. Cleaner

Mathilda also refers to Leon as a "cleaner." As an amusing reference, the bodega near Leon's apartment prominently displays cleaning supplies, like soap, bleach and scouring pads.

10.   A. Milk

Leon regularly buys two quarts of milk from the grocery store, and it is the only beverage he is seen drinking throughout the film.

11.   B. No women, no kids

Mathilda escapes Stansfield and his men because she is at the grocery store. When she returns, she sees the carnage in her family's apartment and walks right past it to Leon's door. Even though he doesn't want to get involved, Leon knows Stansfield will kill Mathilda if he doesn't help. In a way, by not helping Mathilda, he would be violating his "no women, no kids" rule.

QUESTIONS

12. Leon begins to teach Mathilda how to be an assassin, and Mathilda teaches Leon how to what?

    A. Cook
    B. Sing
    C. Dance
    D. Read

13. What is the first weapon Leon teaches Mathilda how to use?

    A. A knife
    B. A pistol
    C. A rifle
    D. A garrote

14. When Leon and Mathilda play charades, which is the only person Leon guesses correctly?

    A. Gene Kelly
    B. Madonna
    C. Marilyn Monroe
    D. Charlie Chaplin

15. What name does Mathilda use when she checks herself and Leon into the hotel?

    A. McGriffin
    B. MacGuffin
    C. Mackenzie
    D. Murphy

ANSWERS

12.   D. Read

Mathilda writes Leon a note saying that she wants to be a cleaner, and tells him to read it. When he stares at it blankly, she realizes he's unable to read. He says he's "had a lot of work lately," so hasn't had time to learn, so Mathilda becomes his teacher.

13.   C. A rifle

Leon gives Mathilda a rifle loaded with paintball pellets, and she practices by "shooting" a jogging politician in Central Park. Afterwards, she asks, "can we try with real bullets now?"

14.   A. Gene Kelly

Mathilda dresses up and acts out the persona of each celebrity, but the only one Leon recognizes is Gene Kelly. Earlier in the film, Leon is alone in a theater enjoying the Gene Kelly movie It's Always Fair Weather, *so he was familiar with the actor. When it's Leon's turn, he impersonates John Wayne, but Mathilda guesses Clint Eastwood.*

15.   B. MacGuffin

"MacGuffin" is a term coined by Alfred Hitchcock to refer to a plot device that serves no purpose other than to move the story forward. In the film, Mathilda says it's the name of a girl in her class "who makes me sick."

QUESTIONS

16. What is the name of the boarding school for troubled girls where Mathilda ends up?

    A. Simpson
    B. Sexton
    C. Spencer
    D. Sandrine

17. What does Mathilda have to remind her of Leon at the end of the film?

    A. His hat
    B. His glasses
    C. A stuffed animal
    D. His plant

18. True or false:

As young as she was, Natalie Portman actually smoked cigarettes in the film to maintain realism.

ANSWERS

16.   C. Spencer

The school is the Spencer School for Girls. At the beginning of the film, Mathilda runs away from the school, and, when the headmistress calls, pretends to be her mother and says she's dead. But after Leon dies, she returns to the school, since it is the only safe haven she has left.

17.   D. His plant

Earlier in the film, Leon tells Mathilda that the plant is his best friend, because it never asks questions and, like him, has no roots. Mathilda thinks that if he really loves the plant, he should plant it in a park so it will have roots. So when she returns to the boarding school, she plants it in front of the school.

18. False

In fact, Portman's parents were so disapproving of the smoking portrayed in the film that they had several conditions: there could be no more than five smoking scenes, Mathilda could never be seen inhaling or exhaling smoke, and her character had to quit smoking during the course of the movie. All of these conditions were met!

TRAINING DAY

1. In the 2001 film *Training Day,* a veteran LAPD narcotics officer trains a rookie for a day. Who directed the film?

     A. Michael Mann
     B. Antoine Fuqua
     C. Guy Ritchie
     D. Christopher Nolan

2. Which actor plays Detective Alonzo Harris?

     A. Samuel L. Jackson
     B. Will Smith
     C. Denzel Washington
     D. Idris Elba

3. Who plays rookie Jake Hoyt?

     A. Ethan Hawke
     B. Matt Damon
     C. Leonardo DiCaprio
     D. Josh Hartnett

ANSWERS

1.   B. Antoine Fuqua

Fuqua's directing credits include Tears of the Sun, King Arthur, Olympus Has Fallen, *and* The Equalizer.

2.   C. Denzel Washington

Washington received an Oscar for Best Actor for his performance in the film, and has said that Alonzo Harris is one of his favorite characters he's ever played.

3.   A. Ethan Hawke

Originally, Hawke's schedule prevented him from signing on to the film, so Tobey Maguire was considered for the part of Hoyt. He even spent two months following LAPD narcotics officers to prepare for the role. But when Hawke's schedule opened up, Maguire was dropped and Hawke was given the part. Poor Tobey!

QUESTIONS

4. Harris and Hoyt begin their morning in a diner, where Hoyt recounts a story for Harris. What is it about?

        A. A drug bust
        B. A bank robbery
        C. A terrorist threat
        D. A DUI stop

5. What kind of car does Harris drive?

        A. Chevy Camaro
        B. Pontiac Firebird
        C. Chevy Monte Carlo
        D. Ford Mustang

6. What animal does Harris compare himself to?

        A. Panther
        B. Lion
        C. Wolf
        D. Fox

7. How does Harris shock Hoyt after their first drug stop?

        A. He throws the drugs away
        B. He forces Hoyt to smoke the drugs
        C. He smokes the drugs himself
        D. He resells the drugs on the street

ANSWERS

4.   D. A DUI stop

Hoyt refuses to be quiet while Harris is reading his morning paper, so Harris demands that he entertain him with a story. Hoyt recalls a DUI stop he made with a previous partner, but Harris is less interested in the details of the story and more interested in details about Hoyt's female partner.

5.   C. Chevy Monte Carlo

Harris' car is a 1979 Chevy Monte Carlo, with a license plate that reads "ORP 967." This was a reference to ex-LAPD officer Rafael Perez, who was born in 1967. Perez stole and resold more than $800,000 of cocaine from evidence lockers, and was accused of being a member of the Bloods gang. The character of Alonzo Harris was based on him.

6.   C. Wolf

Harris repeatedly tells Hoyt that in order to "protect the sheep," they need to act like wolves, because "it takes a wolf to catch a wolf."

7.   B. He forces Hoyt to smoke the drugs

After confiscating what appears to be a small amount of marijuana, Harris tells Hoyt that "a good narcotics agent must love narcotics." He demands that Hoyt smoke the drugs, and after he's done so, Hoyt discovers that the marijuana was laced with PCP.

QUESTIONS

8. What does Hoyt find after saving the girl in the alley from her attackers?

        A. A wallet
        B. A ring
        C. A pair of glasses
        D. A necklace

9. Harris and Hoyt pay a visit to one of Harris' old friends, a retired LAPD officer. What is his name?

        A. Stan
        B. Tim
        C. Roger
        D. Paul

10. What do Harris and Hoyt drink in the car?

        A. Water
        B. Beer
        C. Orange juice
        D. Energy drinks

11. Who plays Blue, a wheelchair-bound drug dealer Hoyt chases into a wig shop?

        A. Dr. Dre
        B. Nelly
        C. Sean Combs
        D. Snoop Dogg

ANSWERS

8. **A. A wallet**

Hoyt finds the girl's pink wallet on the ground. Her school identification is inside, and he learns that she was only 14 years old.

9. **C. Roger**

The part of Roger is played by Scott Glenn, who has appeared in classics like Apocalypse Now, The Right Stuff, The Hunt for Red October, *and* The Silence of the Lambs, *as well as newer blockbusters like* The Bourne Ultimatum *and* The Bourne Legacy.

10. **B. Beer**

In a disturbing example of "kids, don't try this at home," Harris and Hoyt repeatedly drink beer while they drive through the streets of L.A.!

11. **D. Snoop Dogg**

The part of Blue, a drug dealer who tells Harris and Hoyt about his associate, "the Sandman," was a rather small cameo for Snoop Dogg. Dr. Dre appears in a larger role as Paul, a member of Harris' crew. Nelly and Sean Combs both contributed to the soundtrack of the film.

QUESTIONS

12. Which singer plays the Sandman's wife?

    A. Macy Gray
    B. Lauryn Hill
    C. Mariah Carey
    D. Alicia Keys

13. Harris takes Hoyt to a steakhouse for lunch. Who does Harris meet with while he's there?

    A. The Triad
    B. The Three Wise Men
    C. The Ranking Trio
    D. The Cabal

14. What does Harris take from the house of the Sandman's wife?

    A. Drugs
    B. A photo
    C. Money
    D. A gun

15. Which actress plays Harris' girlfriend, Sara?

    A. Eva Mendes
    B. Jessica Alba
    C. Minka Kelly
    D. Olivia Munn

ANSWERS

12.   A. Macy Gray

Training Day *was Gray's film debut. Although best known as a singer, she has since appeared in films including* Domino, Idlewild, *and* The Paperboy, *and on television shows like* American Dreams, That's So Raven, *and* Fuller House.

13.   B. The Three Wise Men

Harris meets with a group of high ranking police officials known as the "Three Wise Men" who turn out to be as corrupt as Harris.

14.   C. Money

Harris steals drug money from the house, and he and Hoyt barely escape when the Sandman's wife alerts gang members to their presence. Later, Harris tells Hoyt he gave the money to the Three Wise Men to procure an unjustified arrest warrant, telling him, "there's nothing free in this world, not even arrest warrants."

15.   A. Eva Mendes

Mendes was not well known before her role in Training Day, *and was actually considering giving up the acting business before she got the part. She has since appeared in dozens of films, including* 2 Fast 2 Furious, Hitch, The Other Guys, *and* The Place Beyond the Pines.

QUESTIONS

16. After paying for the arrest warrant and gathering Harris' crew together, the group goes to whose house?

       A. Paul's
       B. The Sandman's
       C. Harris'
       D. Roger's

17. Harris abandons Hoyt at the house of a gang member named Smiley. What does Smiley tell Hoyt about what Harris did in Las Vegas?

       A. He gambled away his life savings
       B. He killed a member of the Russian mafia
       C. He accidentally got married
       D. He was wanted for a hit and run

18. Why does Smiley decide to let Hoyt live?

       A. He tells Hoyt he can live if he wins at poker
       B. Hoyt tells him he has a daughter and he takes pity on him
       C. Smiley finds out Hoyt saved his cousin
       D. Hoyt promises to pay him a large sum of money

19. True or false:

At the end of the film, Hoyt is shot by one of the residents of the ghetto.

20. True or false:

Harris manages to flee to Mexico at the end of the film.

ANSWERS

16.   D. Roger's

Harris and his gang dig up millions of dollars from underneath Roger's kitchen floor that he made by selling narcotics, then kill Roger and attempt to make it look like justifiable homicide.

17.   B. He killed a member of the Russian mafia

Smiley tells Hoyt that Harris killed a Russian man, who ended up being "a some-body." Because of the incident, he owes the Russian mafia a million dollars before midnight.

18.   C. Smiley finds out Hoyt saved his cousin

In a bit of serendipity, the wallet Hoyt found in the alley after saving the teenager from her attackers turns out to belong to Smiley's cousin. He calls her to ask about the attack, and she confirms that Hoyt was the one who saved her.

19. False

Near the end of the movie, Hoyt has a gun on Harris, and they are surrounded by the residents of the ghetto. Harris announces that he'll pay anyone who shoots Hoyt, but surprisingly, no one reacts. The residents, tired of Harris' arrogance and the way he runs the neighborhood, refuse to do his dirty work for him.

20. False

Reportedly, in the original ending for the film, Harris manages to live. But Washington told The Hollywood Reporter *that "I was not having it." Perhaps audiences wouldn't have reacted well to his villainous character escaping without consequence, so he and Fuqua came up with the new ending where Harris is killed by the Russian mafia in a hail of gunfire.*

THE USUAL
SUSPECTS

1. Who directed the 1995 crime drama *The Usual Suspects?*

    A. Bryan Singer
    B. Martin Scorsese
    C. Christopher Nolan
    D. Sam Mendes

2. The part of Roger "Verbal" Kint is played by which actor?

    A. Christopher Walken
    B. Edward Norton
    C. Kevin Spacey
    D. Steve Buscemi

3. The part of Dave Kujan is played by Chazz Palminteri. But which actor almost played the part?

    A. James Caan
    B. Al Pacino
    C. Robert De Niro
    D. Andy Garcia

ANSWERS

1. A. Bryan Singer

The Usual Suspects *was Singer's first critical success. He has since gone on to helm popular superhero movies like* X-Men, Superman Returns, *and* X-Men: Apocalypse.

2. C. Kevin Spacey

Spacey won the Oscar for Best Actor in a Supporting Role for his part in The Usual Suspects. *Four years later, he won a Best Actor Oscar for* American Beauty.

3. B. Al Pacino

Pacino had to decline due to scheduling conflicts. He has since stated that he regrets not being a part of The Usual Suspects *more than any other film he's turned down.*

QUESTIONS

4. Which government agency does Kujan work for?

    A. U.S. Customs
    B. Central Intelligence Agency
    C. Federal Bureau of Investigations
    D. Drug Enforcement Administration

5. Who plays the part of formerly corrupt ex-cop Dean Keaton?

    A. Gabriel Byrne
    B. Ed Harris
    C. Liam Neeson
    D. Russell Crowe

6. Which Baldwin brother plays the part of Michael McManus, a professional thief?

    A. Alec
    B. Daniel
    C. William
    D. Stephen

7. What is Verbal Kint's disability?

    A. He is blind
    B. He has cerebral palsy
    C. He stutters
    D. He has a prosthetic leg

ANSWERS

4.   A. U.S. Customs

Kujan is a Customs agent who investigates a deadly fire on board a ship docked in San Pedro Bay. Most of the film is told in flashbacks, as Verbal Kint tells his story to Kujan in a cluttered office.

5.   A. Gabriel Byrne

The director kept all his actors in the dark about the identity of Keyser Soze, and Byrne was convinced that his character was the villain. During an interview at a film festival, he said it wasn't until he watched the completed movie that night that he realized it wasn't him!

6.   D. Stephen

Supposedly, Baldwin and his co-star Kevin Pollack (who plays Todd Hockney) began a long-standing feud after filming this movie. Baldwin would reportedly bully the other actors on set in order to stay in character as McManus, which perhaps fueled their animosity.

7.   B. He has cerebral palsy

Spacey talked to doctors before filming to better understand how the condition would affect his character. He also glued together the fingers on his left hand so they'd be unusable, and filed down his shoes so they would match the character's uneven gait.

QUESTIONS

8. Fred Fenster, played by Benicio Del Toro, is McManus' partner. What is unusual about his character?

    A. He is mute
    B. He speaks only Spanish
    C. He speaks in garbled English
    D. He constantly quotes Shakespeare

9. Who is the first of the group to die?

    A. Fenster
    B. McManus
    C. Keaton
    D. Hockney

10. Besides Verbal Kint, there was one other survivor of the massacre on the boat. What is his nationality?

    A. American
    B. Turkish
    C. Italian
    D. Hungarian

11. Who does McManus take the group to see in California?

    A. Redwood
    B. Redfoot
    C. Big Red
    D. Redman

ANSWERS

8.   C. He speaks in garbled English

Del Toro decided to give his character the strange speech inflection because he felt that Fenster's only purpose was to die as an example to the other characters. Nevertheless, co-star Pollack stated that "he stole every scene he was in," even though most of his lines were unintelligible!

9.   A. Fenster

A man named Kobayashi, who says he works for Keyser Soze, claims to have information on all of the criminals and their families. In order to keep their families safe, they must destroy millions of dollars' worth of cocaine on the ship in the harbor. Fenster is killed when he attempts to run away from the job.

10.   D. Hungarian

The only other survivor is a Hungarian criminal named Arkos Kovaz. Because he only speaks Hungarian, it takes some time to translate his interrogation, giving Keyser Soze extra opportunity to slip away.

11.   B. Redfoot

The group goes to see Redfoot, who tells them about a shipment of jewelry to smuggle. When they pull off the heist, they discover that the shipment is heroin, not jewelry. They angrily confront Redfoot, and he tells them that Kobayashi was behind the deception.

QUESTIONS

12. Verbal Kint tells Kujan that he did what in Skokie, Illinois?

    A. Sang in a barbershop quartet
    B. Worked in a library
    C. Visited an apple orchard
    D. Bought orthopedic shoes

13. What nationality is Keyser Soze said to be?

    A. Hungarian
    B. Turkish
    C. Romanian
    D. Polish

14. The film's famous tagline was "Who is Keyser Soze?" Spoiler alert: Who IS Keyser Soze?

    A. Fred Fenster
    B. Dean Keaton
    C. Verbal Kint
    D. Dave Kujan

ANSWERS

12. A. Sang in a barbershop quartet

The screenwriter for The Usual Suspects, *Christopher McQuarrie, states that he was staring at his own bulletin board one day and noticed that it was made by the Quartet company in Skokie, Illinois. The idea struck him to create a character who improvised a story based on items he observed around him. Hence, Verbal Kint and his storytelling ability.*

13. B. Turkish

Supposedly, McQuarrie chose the final name for his character from an English-to-Turkish dictionary.

14. C. Verbal Kint

In what is considered one of the best movie plot twists in cinema history, the unassuming Verbal Kint is revealed to be the criminal mastermind. At the end of the film, Kint limps out of the police station, as Kujan slowly begins to realize that all the details of his story were lifted from objects, flyers, and posters around the cluttered office. By the time Kujan knows that Kint is Keyser Soze, the once-limping man has begun to walk normally. He gets into a car driven by Kobayashi, and the two drive off, never to be seen again.

QUESTIONS

15. True or false:

The film's writer, Christopher McQuarrie, made up all of his character's names off the top of his head, choosing them for no other reason than he liked the way they sounded.

16. True or false:

Film critic Roger Ebert called *The Usual Suspects* "the best film of the year."

17. Finish the line:

"The greatest trick the devil ever pulled was convincing the world _____."

18. Finish the line:

"And like that, _____."

ANSWERS

15. False

The inspiration for the names of the characters came from coworkers at a law firm and a detective agency where McQuarrie worked when he was young. In fact, the name "Keyser Soze" was originally going to be Keyser Sume, the name of McQuarrie's former boss. But after his former boss read the script, he requested the name be slightly changed so he wouldn't be forever associated with an evil criminal.

16. False

Surprisingly, Ebert panned the Oscar-winning film, placing it on his "Most Hated Movies" list and giving it a measly one and a half stars!

17. He didn't exist

The line paraphrases a quote from a poem by French poet Charles Baudelaire. In the film, it is spoken by Verbal Kint, who himself is attempting to convince the police he is someone he's not.

18. He's gone

While being interrogated, Verbal Kint describes the kind of man Keyser Soze is – seemingly a ruthless killer who can disappear at will and leave no trace of his whereabouts. Eerily, McQuarrie based the character of Keyser Soze on real-life killer John List, who murdered his family and then disappeared for 18 years. When he was finally captured, List was living a new life under the name Robert Peter Clark. In the film, "And like that, he's gone," is the final line spoken, giving the viewer the sense that Keyser Soze is, once again, in the wind.

21 JUMP STREET

1. The film *21 Jump Street* is based on the television show of the same name that debuted in what year?

    A. 1985
    B. 1986
    C. 1987
    D. 1988

2. Which actor plays Morton Schmidt, an intelligent yet socially awkward police officer?

    A. Jonah Hill
    B. Chris Hemsworth
    C. Jesse Eisenberg
    D. Adam DeVine

3. Who plays Greg Jenko, Schmidt's slow-witted yet strong partner?

    A. Charlie Hunnam
    B. Channing Tatum
    C. Chris Pine
    D. Tom Hardy

ANSWERS

1.   C. 1987

The show ran from 1987 to 1991. Reportedly, star Johnny Depp signed an extended contract for the show only because he thought it would be a failure after one season and then he would be free to pursue other projects. Ironically, it was Depp's appearance on the show that made it such a hit.

2.   A. Jonah Hill

Hill also co-wrote the script for the film, which he described as "an R-rated, insane, Bad Boys-meets-John-Hughes-type movie."

3.   B. Channing Tatum

Tatum's character is named after Captain Richard Jenko on the original television series, played by actor Frederic Forrest.

QUESTIONS

4. Which rapper plays the police captain who manages 21 Jump Street?

      A. Ice-T
      B. Common
      C. Ice Cube
      D. Ludacris

5. In the opening scenes of the movie, who does Schmidt bear a resemblance to?

      A.Jerry Seinfeld
      B. Eminem
      C. Will Smith
      D. Michael Jackson

6. What happened to Jenko as a result of his poor grades in high school?

      A. He is barred from the prom
      B. He never graduates
      C. He has help clean blackboards
      D. He gets a month of detention

7. What is the name of the motorcycle gang the duo confronts at the beginning of the film?

      A. Roadside Rebels
      B. Sons of Bandidos
      C. One-Percenters
      D. Freedom Fighters

ANSWERS

4.   C. Ice Cube

Apparently Ice Cube's tough guy persona wasn't entirely an act. According to Hill, it is extremely difficult to make the actor laugh. While Hill and Tatum were continually cracking up on set, they were unable to coerce so much as a smile from the hip-hop artist!

5.   B. Eminem

At the beginning of the film, we see a high-school-aged Schmidt with his hair dyed blond and cut in the style of Eminem during his "Real Slim Shady" era. According to Hill, this was not just a gag for the film. He says, "This is what I actually looked like in high school!"

6.   A. He is barred from the prom

Whereas awkward Schmidt attempts to ask a girl to the prom and fails, Jenko is barred altogether due to his poor academic performance. Later, the duo would attend their first prom as undercover students.

7.   C. One-Percenters

Schmidt and Jenko get so excited about the prospect of arresting the One-Percenters' gang leader, Domingo (played by DeRay Davis), that they forget to read him his Miranda Rights and the police are forced to release him.

QUESTIONS

8. What kind of building is located at 21 Jump Street?

    A. An abandoned theater
    B. A gymnasium
    C. An empty warehouse
    D. A church

9. Which cast member from the original television show has a cameo as the officer who gives Schmidt and Jenko a car?

    A. Holly Robinson Peete
    B. Dustin Nguyen
    C. Sal Jenco
    D. Yvette Nipar

10. When they get to the high school, Schmidt and Jenko discover that Schmidt is now the "cool" one and Jenko is the outcast. What does Jenko blame for the reversal?

    A. *High School Musical*
    B. *Glee*
    C. *American Idol*
    D. *The Big Bang Theory*

11. What are Schmidt and Jenko's undercover names?

    A. John and Doug
    B. Brad and Joe
    C. Joe and John
    D. Doug and Brad

ANSWERS

8.   D. A church

The Korean church, called the Aroma of Christ Church, houses the headquarters at 21 Jump Street. This is similar to the original series, where the undercover squad is located in an abandoned chapel dubbed "Jump Street Chapel."

9.   A. Holly Robinson Peete

Peete, who was the only cast member to stay with the show through its entire run, reprises her role as Officer Judy Hoffs in the film.

10.   B. *Glee*

Jenko discovers that his tough jock persona is no longer appreciated among the students, whereas Schmidt's geekiness is embraced. Confused, Jenko proclaims that Glee *must be to blame.*

11.   D. Doug and Brad

Schmidt and Jenko go undercover as Doug and Brad McQuaid. In the original television series, Johnny Depp's and Peter DeLuise's characters also posed as "the McQuaid brothers" in several episodes.

QUESTIONS

12. Which award-winning actress appears as high schooler Molly Tracey?

    A. Jennifer Lawrence
    B. Brie Larson
    C. Emmy Rossum
    D. Carey Mulligan

13. Who plays Eric Molson, one of the high school drug dealers?

    A. Dave Franco
    B. John Francis Daley
    C. Colton Haynes
    D. Zac Efron

14. What class is Jenko enrolled in that he is surprised to discover he likes?

    A. American History
    B. AP English
    C. Biology
    D. AP Chemistry

15. After Schmidt makes contact with Eric the dealer, where do they meet to buy the drugs?

    A. A janitor's closet
    B. The yearbook office
    C. The bathroom
    D. Behind the football field

ANSWERS

12.   B. Brie Larson

Larson won a Best Actress Oscar in 2016 for her portrayal of "Ma" in Room.

13.   A. Dave Franco

Franco is, of course, the brother of actor James Franco. He has stated that he attempts to "distance himself" from his famous older brother to prove he can stand on his own two feet as an actor.

14.   D. AP Chemistry

Schmidt and Jenko fail to memorize their respective aliases, and accidentally end up switching their "Doug" and "Brad" personas. As a result, Jenko ends up in the AP Chemistry class that Schmidt was supposed to take, and Schmidt ends up in Jenko's drama class.

15.   B. The yearbook office

Eric forces Schmidt and Jenko to take the drugs in the yearbook office before they leave, and the two endure all the phases of the drug, including "over-falsity of confidence" and "asleepyness."

QUESTIONS

16. For which musical does Schmidt audition and win the lead?

    A. *Peter Pan*
    B. *Brigadoon*
    C. *Carousel*
    D. *Oklahoma*

17. Who does the drug supplier surprisingly turn out to be?

    A. Mr. Gordon, the drama teacher
    B. Mr. Walters, the P.E. teacher
    C. Ms. Griggs, the chemistry teacher
    D. Principal Dadier

18. What does Jenko write a poem about that he recites in front of his class?

    A. H2O
    B. Sodium Nitrate
    C. Potassium Nitrate
    D. Sodium Chloride

19. Which two stars of the original television series have uncredited cameos as undercover officers?

    A. Johnny Depp and Sal Jenko
    B. Dustin Nguyen and Peter DeLuise
    C. Johnny Depp and Peter DeLuise
    D. Johnny Depp and Richard Grieco

20. How does Jenko thwart the pursuing motorcycle gang in the limo?

    A. Makes a bomb
    B. Shoots their tires
    C. Takes the wheel and outruns them
    D. Creates a makeshift smokescreen

ANSWERS

16.   A. *Peter Pan*

Schmidt performs his audition during the "over-falsity of confidence" phase of his drug trip and manages to win the lead of Peter Pan. His new friend Molly is given the part of Wendy.

17.   B. Mr. Walters, the P.E. teacher

Earlier in the film, there's a subtle clue that Mr. Walters, played by Rob Riggle, is the supplier. When Schmidt and Jenko try the drug, Jenko remarks that it tastes like "cool ranch." When they run into Mr. Walters a little while later, he is carrying a bag of Cool Ranch Doritos.

18.   C. Potassium Nitrate

Jenko, embracing his new love of science, wears a jacket emblazoned with "KNO3," the chemical symbol for potassium nitrate, and recites a poem with lines like, "Potassium nitrate. Don't hate. It's great. It can act as an oxidizer. I didn't know that, but now I'm wiser."

19.   C. Johnny Depp and Peter DeLuise

Depp and DeLuise appear as their original characters, Tom Hanson and Doug Penhall. Unfortunately, both of the parts are short-lived, as their characters are shot by the One-Percenters.

20.   A. Makes a bomb

Once again using his newfound chemistry knowledge, Jenko creates a bomb with tequila, potassium nitrate from shotgun shells, and lithium. He then throws it into the open sunroof of the gang's limo. Hooray for science!

THE DAY THE EARTH STOOD STILL

1. *The Day the Earth Stood Still* centers around an alien who visits Earth. What is the alien's name?

    A. Kamut
    B. Klabu
    C. Klaatu
    D. Kamata

2. In what year was the original film released?

    A. 1951
    B. 1952
    C. 1954
    D. 1958

3. Which actor plays the alien in the 2008 remake?

    A. Matthew McConaughey
    B. Keanu Reeves
    C. Adrien Brody
    D. Michael Fassbender

ANSWERS

1.   C. Klaatu

In the original film, British actor Michael Rennie plays the part of Klaatu. Since he was relatively unknown to American audiences, the filmmakers thought he would make a believable alien.

2.   A. 1951

The movie was based on a short story by writer Harry Bates called "Farewell to the Master." 20th Century Fox paid him only $500 for the rights to the story.

3.   B. Keanu Reeves

Reeves was the first and only choice for the part. He has stated that his own favorite movie remake is the 1978 film Invasion of the Body Snatchers.

QUESTIONS

4. The director of the original film, Robert Wise, also directed which beloved classic?

      A. *Mary Poppins*
      B. *Lawrence of Arabia*
      C. *The Sound of Music*
      D. *Breakfast at Tiffany's*

5. Which modern-day composer was so inspired by the score of the 1951 film that he became a composer himself?

      A. Howard Shore
      B. James Horner
      C. Alan Silvestri
      D. Danny Elfman

6. Where does the alien ship land in the 2008 version of the film?

      A. New York
      B. Boston
      C. Los Angeles
      D. San Francisco

7. What is the name of the robot who accompanies the alien to Earth?

      A. Gert
      B. Gort
      C. Gary
      D. Gorp

ANSWERS

4.   C. *The Sound of Music*

Wise won Oscars for Best Picture and Best Director for the film. He also won Best Picture and Best Director Oscars for 1961's West Side Story.

5.   D. Danny Elfman

Elfman loved composer Bernard Herrmann's score, which made unique use of a Theremin, one of the earliest electronic musical instruments ever invented. The film is one of the first to have a mostly electronic score.

6.   A. New York

In the original film, the ship lands in Washington D.C., but in the remake, the ship lands in New York City's Central Park.

7.   B. Gort

In the original film, Gort was only 8 feet tall. But with the help of CGI, he became a 28-foot-tall robot in the remake. In the newer version, "GORT" is said to stand for "genetically organized robotic technology." The robot eventually transforms itself into tiny nanobots which destroy everything in their path.

QUESTIONS

8. The famous line, "Klaatu barada nikto" is used in both films. What is its purpose?

        A. It is a greeting
        B. It makes the alien ship fly
        C. It stops the robot from attacking humans
        D. It describes the alien's intentions for Earth

9. In the original film, actress Patricia Neal plays the part of Helen Benson, who befriends the alien and helps him with his mission. Which actress plays the part in the remake?

        A. Rachel Weisz
        B. Jennifer Connelly
        C. Natalie Portman
        D. Anne Hathaway

10. In the remake, what is Helen Benson's profession?

        A. Astrophysicist
        B. Astronomer
        C. Biochemist
        D. Astrobiologist

11. In the original movie, Helen has a son named Bobby, played by actor Billy Gray. In which popular '50s television show did Gray star?

        A. *Father Knows Best*
        B. *Leave It to Beaver*
        C. *Lassie*
        D. *The Adventures of Ozzie and Harriet*

ANSWERS

8.   C. It stops the robot from attacking humans

The line is also used in the cult favorite film Army of Darkness, *where Bruce Campbell's character, Ash, must use the words to stop the army of the undead.*

9.   B. Jennifer Connelly

Connelly doesn't often appear in sci-fi films, but she said the story intrigued her, and she "liked that it was a movie that gave a truthful view to where we are as a planet."

10.   D. Astrobiologist

This is a fitting job for her character, since an astrobiologist studies the possibility of life in other parts of the universe.

11.   A. *Father Knows Best*

Gray was a prolific child actor, appearing in his first film when he was only five years old. He would go on to have parts in dozens of movies and television shows before landing the role of Bud Anderson on Father Knows Best.

QUESTIONS

12. Who plays Helen's son, Jacob, in the remake?

    A. Josh Hutcherson
    B. Asa Butterfield
    C. Jaden Smith
    D. Liam James

13. What name does the alien assume when he takes refuge at the boarding house in the original film?

    A. Mr. Carpenter
    B. Mr. Cooper
    C. Mr. Kendrick
    D. Mr. Kipling

14. In the original film, the part of Professor Barnhardt is played by actor Sam Jaffe. Who plays the part in the remake?

    A. Anthony Hopkins
    B. John Cleese
    C. Gary Oldman
    D. John Turturro

15. In the 2008 version, when Helen asks the alien, "Are you a friend to us?" how does he respond?

    A. "That depends."
    B. "Not to all of you."
    C. "I'm a friend to the Earth."
    D. "Yes."

ANSWERS

12.   C. Jaden Smith

Jaden's dad is actor Will Smith, who, incidentally, turned down the role of Neo in The Matrix. *That part of course went to Keanu Reeves, who appears with Jaden in* The Day the Earth Stood Still.

13.   A. Mr. Carpenter

Klaatu steals a suit from a hospital's dry cleaner so he can blend in with the humans. He sees the name on the tag and borrows it for himself.

14.   B. John Cleese

The filmmakers were hesitant to cast Cleese at first, since he is known more for his comedic roles and "Monty Python" humor. But they reportedly enjoyed working with him so much, they were sorry when filming ended!

15.   C. "I'm a friend to the Earth."

To Helen's dismay, she discovers that Klaatu's mission is to eradicate humanity and their destructive ways, while preserving the Earth.

QUESTIONS

16. In the original movie, the alien asks Bobby who the greatest man in America is. Who does Bobby suggest?

    A. Professor Barnhardt
    B. The President
    C. His father
    D. James Dean

17. What does the alien ultimately have to use to prevent the destruction of humanity in the 2008 film?

    A. A laser
    B. An EMP
    C. A nuclear bomb
    D. An invisible shield

18. True or false:

In the original film, camera angles and a clever costume were used to make Gort appear almost 8 feet tall.

ANSWERS

16.   A. Professor Barnhardt

Bobby and Klaatu visit the professor's home, but he is not there. Perhaps to intrigue the professor and convince him to meet, Klaatu completes a complex equation the professor has written on a blackboard, and then leaves his contact information with the housekeeper.

17.   B. An EMP

Helen and Jacob manage to convince Klaatu that humans are worth saving, so at the end of the film, he walks through the destructive nanobots and touches his ship, which emits an EMP. This destroys the nanobots, but it also destroys all of the technology on earth.

18. False

The actor who played Gort, Lock Martin, was one of the tallest actors who has even been on screen, at a reported 7 feet 7 inches tall. He towered over even his 6'3" co-star, Michael Rennie, and was nearly a full two feet taller than actress Patricia Neal.

FOOTLOOSE

1. Kevin Bacon plays the part of Ren MacCormack in the original 1984 version of *Footloose*. Which city does Ren live in before moving to the small-town Midwest?

    A. New York
    B. Los Angeles
    C. Chicago
    D. Dallas

2. The 2011 version of the film starred a dancer who toured with Justin Timberlake. What is his name?

    A. Kenny Wormald
    B. Channing Tatum
    C. Chris Messina
    D. Taylor Lautner

3. Which big city does Ren hail from in the remake?

    A. Boston
    B. Miami
    C. San Diego
    D. Seattle

ANSWERS

1.   C. Chicago

John Travolta, well known at the time for his dancing moves in movies like Saturday Night Fever *and* Grease, *was offered the part of the Chicago boy who moves to a small town, but he turned it down. Ren became an iconic role for Kevin Bacon.*

2.   A. Kenny Wormald

Wormald was born in 1984, the same year the original movie was released. He has been dancing since he was six years old, and Timberlake himself recommended him for the part because of his professional experience.

3.   A. Boston

Wormald is from Boston and has a strong accent. So Footloose *director Craig Brewer changed Ren's original city from Chicago to Boston and encouraged Wormald to hang on to his accent.*

QUESTIONS

4. Who sings the famous theme song "Footloose"?

    A. Christopher Cross
    B. Hall & Oates
    C. Kenny Loggins
    D. Kenny Rogers

5. Both film versions center around an ultra-religious minister named Reverend Shaw Moore who bans dancing in his small town. Which actor plays Rev. Moore in the original film?

    A. John Lithgow
    B. Ed Harris
    C. William Hurt
    D. John Heard

6. Who plays Rev. Moore in the remake?

    A. Scott Bakula
    B. Nicholas Cage
    C. Kevin Costner
    D. Dennis Quaid

7. Which actress plays Ariel, Rev. Moore's daughter, in the 1984 version?

    A. Corinne Bohrer
    B. Lori Singer
    C. Mia Sara
    D. Ione Skye

ANSWERS

4.   C. Kenny Loggins

The film opens with a shot of dozens of dancing feet, set to the upbeat song. The feet with the gold shoes actually belong to Loggins himself.

5.   A. John Lithgow

When Rev. Moore shows Ren a picture of his deceased son, it is actually a photo of Lithgow's real son.

6.   D. Dennis Quaid

One review said that Quaid's Rev. Moore "is a flawed man, racked more by the loss of a son than anger toward the dance."

7.   B. Lori Singer

Singer was 27 years old when the film was released, but she played a high school senior. In fact, she was only nine years younger than her on-screen mother, Dianne Wiest!

QUESTIONS

8. Who plays Ariel in the 2011 film?

    A. Amy Adams
    B. Zoe Saldana
    C. Julianne Hough
    D. Amanda Schull

9. Who plays the part of Willard, Ren's best friend, in the 1984 film?

    A. Kevin James
    B. John C. Reilly
    C. Chris Penn
    D. Jon Cryer

10. In the remake, Willard is played by which *Divergent* actor?

    A. Miles Teller
    B. Theo James
    C. Jai Courtney
    D. Ansel Elgort

11. Ariel's best friend, Rusty, is played by Ziah Colon in the remake. Which award-winning actress plays the part in the original film?

    A. Diane Lane
    B. Sarah Jessica Parker
    C. Kyra Sedgwick
    D. Jami Gertz

ANSWERS

8. C. Julianne Hough

The Dancing with the Stars *alum beat out Hayden Panettiere, Miley Cyrus, and Amanda Bynes for the part of Ariel.*

9. C. Chris Penn

Penn, who sadly passed away in 2006, was the brother of Sean Penn. He really didn't know how to dance, so the script was modified to show his character learning to dance.

10. A. Miles Teller

Teller, best known for his role as Peter in the Divergent *series, actually played the part of Willard in a high school production of* Footloose: The Musical.

11. B. Sarah Jessica Parker

Parker won an Emmy and four Golden Globes for her role as Carrie Bradshaw on the HBO series Sex and the City.

QUESTIONS

12. What is the incident that leads to the anti-dancing stance in the town in both films?

    A. A bullied student
    B. A drug overdose
    C. A car accident
    D. A balcony collapse

13. What is the name of Ariel's abusive boyfriend?

    A. Travis
    B. Chuck
    C. Andy
    D. Rich

14. What song is playing when Ren teaches Willard to dance?

    A. "Let's Hear It for the Boy"
    B. "Holding Out for a Hero"
    C. "Dancing in the Street"
    D. "Wake Me Up Before You Go-Go"

15. What is the name for the secret location that Ariel takes Ren?

    A. The Clubhouse
    B. The Yard
    C. The Passage
    D. The Yearbook

ANSWERS

12.   C. A car accident

Ariel's brother died in a car accident after a night of drinking and dancing. As a result, Rev. Moore, grieving over the loss of his son, convinces the town council to ban all forms of partying and dancing.

13.   B. Chuck

In the original film, a jealous Chuck challenges Ren to a tractor race when he senses the chemistry between Ren and Ariel. In the 2011 film, Chuck challenges Ren to race old buses.

14.   A. "Let's Hear It for the Boy"

The song, performed by Deniece Williams, was used in both films for the same scene.

15.   D. The Yearbook

"The Yearbook" turns out to be an abandoned train car, where the high school kids write quotes and poetry on the walls.

QUESTIONS

16. True or false:

To this day, Kevin Bacon loves to hear the song "Footloose," and often breaks out dancing when he hears it.

17. True or false:

Footloose was loosely based on real events.

18. True or false:

The original 1984 film was an immediate hit.

ANSWERS

16. False

Bacon has actually gone so far as to tip DJs NOT to play the song. He says that even though he performed some of the dancing moves himself, much of his dancing in the film was performed by Peter Tramm, his dance double.

17. True

The story was inspired by events in the small farming town of Elmore City, Oklahoma. Dancing had been banned in the town since its founding in 1861, but in 1978 a group of high schoolers was able to get the ban overturned and they won the right to dance at their prom.

18. False

The film, now considered a classic, was received rather lukewarmly. Critic Roger Ebert called it "a seriously confused movie" and "a collection of unrelated ingredients that someone thought would be exploitable."

OCEAN'S ELEVEN

1. Who plays Danny Ocean in the original 1960 version of *Ocean's Eleven*?

    A. Peter Lawford
    B. Frank Sinatra
    C. Cesar Romero
    D. Cary Grant

2. Who plays Danny Ocean in the 2001 remake?

    A. Matt Damon
    B. Ben Affleck
    C. Brad Pitt
    D. George Clooney

3. Both films include an impressive lineup of popular stars. Who does NOT appear in the original film?

    A. Dean Martin
    B. Sammy Davis Jr.
    C. Perry Como
    D. Red Skelton

ANSWERS

1.   B. Frank Sinatra

Sinatra, whose nicknames include "The Voice," "Chairman of the Board," and of course, "Ol' Blue Eyes," was one of the most popular singers in the world at the time. He won a Best Supporting Actor Oscar in 1954 for From Here to Eternity.

2.   D. George Clooney

Reportedly, Bruce Willis was the original choice for Danny Ocean, but he had to decline due to scheduling conflicts. He makes a cameo appearance in the sequel, Ocean's Twelve.

3.   C. Perry Como

Perry Como is not in the original film. However, he can be heard performing "Papa Loves Mambo" on the soundtrack of the 2001 remake.

QUESTIONS

4. Which Oscar winner directed the 2001 version?

A. Sam Mendes
B. Robert Zemeckis
C. Steven Soderbergh
D. Danny Boyle

5. In the original film, how do the pals know each other?

A. They work together in a factory
B. They're all cousins
C. They don't – they just met
D. They fought together in the war

6. In the 2001 version, Julia Roberts plays Danny Ocean's estranged wife, Tess. In the 1960 version, Ocean's wife is named Beatrice and is played by which actress?

A. Angie Dickinson
B. Barbara Eden
C. Mitzi Gaynor
D. Kim Novak

7. The casinos targeted in the original film are the Sahara, Riviera, Desert Inn, Sands, and The Flamingo. Which casinos are targeted in the 2001 film?

A. Wynn, Bellagio, Caesar's Palace
B. Bellagio, Mirage, MGM Grand
C. Palazzo, Mirage, Wynn
D. Bellagio, Mirage, Venetian

ANSWERS

4.   C. Steven Soderbergh

Soderbergh won an Oscar for Best Director in 2000 for Traffic. *He originally wanted to film* Ocean's Eleven *in black and white, but was told he could only do so if he reduced the cost to make the movie.*

5.   D. They fought together in the war

The group fought together in World War II in the 82nd Airborne division.

6.   A. Angie Dickinson

Dickinson appears again in the 2001 version. She has a cameo as a spectator at the boxing match.

7.   B. Bellagio, Mirage, MGM Grand

Of the original five casinos, only The Flamingo remains intact. The Riviera, Desert Inn, and Sands are permanently closed, and The Sahara was transformed into the SLS Hotel and Casino in 2014.

QUESTIONS

8. Who is the last man to be recruited into the group in the 2001 film?

    A. Rusty
    B. Saul
    C. Linus
    D. Yen

9. Which actress has an uncredited cameo as a drunk girl in the original film?

    A. Sophia Loren
    B. Tina Louise
    C. Florence Henderson
    D. Shirley MacLaine

10. In the remake, what is the name of the man, played by Andy Garcia, who owns the casinos that the group robs?

    A. Terry Benedict
    B. Roman Nagel
    C. Willy Bank
    D. Gaspar LeMarque

11. What does Basher Tarr call the device he uses to knock out the power in the city?

    A. Pop
    B. Pinch
    C. Wave
    D. Squeeze

ANSWERS

8. C. Linus

Linus, played by Matt Damon, is a pickpocket Danny finds in Chicago. He watches Linus steal a man's wallet on the train, and then surreptitiously slips a card into Linus' pocket telling him where to meet so he can recruit him to his team.

9. D. Shirley MacLaine

MacLaine adlibbed her part for the film, and reportedly received a new car from Warner Bros. as compensation for her work.

10. A. Terry Benedict

While he is being robbed, Benedict is handed a piece of paper that shows him the amount of money in his vaults: $163,156,759.

11. B. Pinch

The "pinch" was based on an actual device called a "z-pinch," however, the movie took quite a few liberties with the science. A real "pinch" would be too big to fit in a van, would need a very large power source, and wouldn't be nearly powerful enough to knock out the power in a city.

QUESTIONS

12. What is the classical music piece that plays after the gang pulls off their heist in the 2001 film?

        A. *The Four Seasons* by Vivaldi
        B. *Liebestraum* by Liszt
        C. *Clair de Lune* by Debussy
        D. *Raindrop Prelude* by Chopin

13. Who is the last of the group to walk away from the fountains at the end of the remake?

        A. Saul
        B. Linus
        C. Danny
        D. Rusty

14. In the final shot of the original film, the group walks past the sign of which hotel?

        A. The Flamingo
        B. The Sands
        C. The Sahara
        D. The Tropicana

ANSWERS

12.   **C. *Clair de Lune* by Debussy**

The music actually "bookends" the caper, as the piece is also playing at the pool party immediately before they begin to plan the robbery.

13.   **A. Saul**

The director allowed the actors to mostly improvise the scene by the fountain, asking only that Rusty leave first and Saul leave last. Everyone else was told to do whatever seemed right.

14.   **B. The Sands**

As the group walks past the Sands hotel sign, the names of Frank Sinatra, Dean Martin, Sammy Davis Jr., Joey Bishop, and Peter Lawford – The Rat Pack – can all be seen. They were all performing at the hotel during the film's production.

QUESTIONS

15. True or false:

Topher Grace, Joshua Jackson, and Don Cheadle all have uncredited roles in the 2001 film.

16. True or false:

In the 1960 film, one of the main characters dies.

17. True or false:

All of the main actors in the 1960 film stayed together at the same hotel during filming.

ANSWERS

15. True

While Grace and Jackson have brief cameos, Cheadle plays a major role as Basher Tarr, so it's unusual that he is uncredited. There was a dispute over the order in which his name would appear in the billing, with Cheadle wanting his name to appear before the title along with George Clooney, Brad Pitt, and Matt Damon. When the filmmakers refused to do this, Cheadle chose not to be credited at all. He got his wish for Ocean's Twelve *and* Ocean's Thirteen, *where his name appears before the titles of the films.*

16. True

While both versions share comedic elements, the 1960 version takes a sadder turn when one of the 11, Tony Bergdorf, played by actor Richard Conte, dies of a heart attack. The rest of the gang hides their stolen money in his casket, only to discover that Bergdorf's widow has decided to have his body cremated, along with all of the hidden money!

17. False

In a sad sign of the times, Sammy Davis Jr. was forced to stay at a "colored only" hotel during filming, even though he was one of the headliners at the Sands along with his co-stars. Black artists were also barred from gambling in the casinos or eating or drinking at any of the hotel restaurants. Frank Sinatra was incensed by the way his friend was being treated, and threatened to quit performing in shows at the Sands unless Davis was given the same accommodations as everyone else. This paved the way for other black performers, and the color barrier in Las Vegas was finally broken.

THE PARENT TRAP

1. What year was the original version of *The Parent Trap* released?

    A. 1960
    B. 1961
    C. 1962
    D. 1963

2. In *The Parent Trap,* a set of identical twins, unaware of the other's existence, meet at summer camp and conspire to reunite their divorced parents. Which actress plays the part of twins Susan and Sharon in the original film?

    A. Sally Field
    B. Peggy Lipton
    C. Hayley Mills
    D. Patty Duke

3. Who plays the part of the twins, named Annie and Hallie, in the 1998 remake?

    A. Amanda Bynes
    B. Brittany Snow
    C. Mary-Kate and Ashley Olsen
    D. Lindsay Lohan

ANSWERS

1.   B. 1961

The film was nominated for two Oscars, for Best Sound and Best Film Editing, and also received a Golden Globe nomination for Best Motion Picture.

2.   C. Hayley Mills

Mills received a Golden Globe nomination for Best Actress for her dual role. While she alone is credited for both parts, actress Susan Henning stood in as her body double in many shots in the film where both twins were on screen.

3.   D. Lindsay Lohan

This was 11-year-old Lohan's first film. Nancy Meyers, who also had her first directing credit with The Parent Trap, *hand-picked her for the role.*

QUESTIONS

4. Which popular actress of the '40s, '50s, and '60s plays the twins' mother, Maggie McKendrick, in the original film?

    A. Lauren Bacall
    B. Shelley Winters
    C. Maureen O'Hara
    D. Joan Fontaine

5. In the remake, who plays the father of the twins, Nick Parker?

    A. Dennis Quaid
    B. Kevin Costner
    C. Steve Carell
    D. James Belushi

6. What is the name of the summer camp the girls attend in the original film?

    A. Camp Pine
    B. Camp Inch
    C. Camp Mile
    D. Camp Woods

7. When the girls are at camp, what cabin are they in when they discover they are twins?

    A. The arts and crafts cabin
    B. The cafeteria
    C. The isolation cabin
    D. The counselors' cabin

8. What is the name of the camp the girls attend in the 1998 version of the film?

    A. Camp Walden
    B. Camp Wisteria
    C. Camp Thoreau
    D. Camp Wildwood

ANSWERS

4.   C. Maureen O'Hara

O'Hara, known for her trademark red hair, starred in classics like How Green Was My Valley, Miracle on 34th Street, *and* The Quiet Man. *She worked alongside actor Brian Keith, who plays the twins' father, Mitch.*

5.   A. Dennis Quaid

Quaid has stated that Lohan was a "natural" in her part, and was "a talented, talented kid." Her onscreen mom, Elizabeth, is played by Natasha Richardson.

6.   B. Camp Inch

The camp is run by Miss Inch, who calls herself the "supreme commander" of the camp. She is played by Ruth McDevitt, who also appeared in The Birds *and* Mame.

7.   C. The isolation cabin

The girls are sent to the "isolation cabin" for causing shenanigans (or, as Miss Inch calls it, "hooliganism"). It is there that they finally discover they have the same parents and their identical looks are no coincidence.

8.   A. Camp Walden

The camp was based on an actual camp for girls, of the same name, that is still in operation in the town of Denmark, Maine.

QUESTIONS

9. What is the name of the restaurant in the original film where Maggie and Mitch had their first date?

    A. Machiavelli's
    B. Murano's
    C. Martinelli's
    D. Mario's

10. Where do Annie and Elizabeth live in the remake?

    A. New York
    B. Los Angeles
    C. Rome
    D. London

11. Which *Friends* alum has a role as camp counselor Marva Kulp Jr. in the 1998 film?

    A. Lisa Kudrow
    B. Maggie Wheeler
    C. Jane Sibbett
    D. Lauren Tom

12. What is the name of Mitch's "gold digger" fiancée in the original film?

    A. Louise
    B. Edna
    C. Vicki
    D. Betsy

13. What is the name of the song that Susan and Sharon sing for their parents on their recreated first date in the original movie?

    A. "Let's Get Together"
    B. "Side by Side"
    C. "We're Two of a Kind"
    D. "You and Me"

ANSWERS

9.   C. Martinelli's

Susan and Sharon conspire to recreate their parents' first date at Martinelli's Italian restaurant, complete with "the drippy candles, the violin music," and "the veal parmesan."

10.   D. London

Elizabeth is a successful wedding dress designer, raising Annie in London, while Nick raises Hallie in Napa Valley, where he owns a vineyard.

11.   B. Maggie Wheeler

Wheeler is probably best known for her role as Janice on Friends. *Her character in* The Parent Trap *was named after actress Nancy Kulp, who played a camp counselor in the original film.*

12.   C. Vicki

Vicki was played by actress Joanna Barnes. In the remake, Barnes makes an appearance as the mother of Nick's "gold digger" fiancé, Meredith, played by Elaine Hendrix.

13.   A. "Let's Get Together"

The song was written specifically for the film by Robert and Richard Sherman. Incidentally, in the 1998 remake, Lindsay Lohan can be heard singing the same song as she gets into the elevator at the hotel.

QUESTIONS

14. What are the two smells that remind the girls of their grandfather?

    A. Cinnamon and vanilla
    B. Peppermint and tobacco
    C. Vanilla and coffee
    D. Chocolate and orange

15. How do Hallie and Nick manage to beat Elizabeth and Annie back to London at the end of the 1998 film?

    A. Elizabeth and Annie's flight gets cancelled
    B. Hallie and Nick rent a private jet
    C. Elizabeth and Annie return by boat
    D. Hallie and Nick take the Concorde

16. Which singer's love songs are featured in the opening and closing scenes of the remake?

    A. Perry Como
    B. Ella Fitzgerald
    C. Nat King Cole
    D. Elvis Presley

17. True or false:

The girls in the remake were named after the director's daughters.

18. True or false:

The original version of *The Parent Trap* was the first film to make use of split screen technology.

ANSWERS

14.   B. Peppermint and tobacco

In the original film, Susan's grandfather tells her that the peppermint is "for my indigestion" and the tobacco is "to make your grandmother mad." Hallie smells the same scents on her grandfather in the remake.

15.   D. Hallie and Nick take the Concorde

The Concorde was a supersonic passenger jet that could fly at twice the speed of sound, making the transatlantic flight between New York and London in the half the time of a regular jet. Sadly, Concorde flights were permanently discontinued in 2003.

16.   C. Nat King Cole

Cole's song "L.O.V.E" plays in the beginning when we see scenes of Elizabeth and Nick's first wedding, and "This Will Be (An Everlasting Love)" plays at the end, over shots of their second wedding.

17. True

Director Nancy Meyers and producer Charles Shyer have two daughters together, Annie and Hallie, and the characters in the film were named after them. The real Annie and Hallie have cameo roles in the film, as a towel girl at the hotel and a camper at Camp Walden.

18. False

Surprisingly, split screen technology has been employed in filmmaking since the 1890s. But The Parent Trap was the first successful blockbuster to use it. The split screens were concealed with things like tent poles, doorframes, and bedposts, and footprints were drawn on the floor of the set so Hayley Mills would know where she needed to stand in order to create a seamless finished scene. The filmmakers even made use of a metronome in order to time beats when Mills walked, so she would know exactly when to look to her left or right at her "twin." Although Walt Disney was pleased with the finished product, the process wasn't completely without flaws. Occasionally the seam in the frame is noticeable, as in the "Let's Get Together" scene when the "twin" on the left loses an arm for a split second during the song routine!